Praise for *Being God's Child*

'In their everyday moments, children a
God – what a lovely insight and promp'
Hannah Persaud, Growing Faith netwo

'Anna invites us on to a journey… where there's freedom to play and grow. *Being God's Child* is a "pick and mix", with ideas rather than chapters so you can dip in to whatever is helpful.'
Sammy Jordan, director of Hope for Every Home

'Anna calls us to see God in the middle of our family life and learn from our kids how to be God's child more and more. A fantastic book for all parents who are looking to connect with God in the midst of parenting.'
Rachel Turner, founder of Parenting for Faith

'*Being God's Child* helps busy parents (and which parent is not busy!) springboard from their role as parent into their role as a child of God. Decide to dwell deeper with God by dipping into this book and trying out the ideas suggested.'
Olly Goldenberg, founder of Children Can

'Anna lifts our eyes to see that in our heavenly Father's care, we can find peace, rest and purpose in our parenting.'
Ed Drew, founder of Faith in Kids

'Full of Bible-based and Christ-centred wisdom, signposts and safe places to land.'
Liz Hall, deputy director family ministries department, The Salvation Army

'A joyous journey… embracing Jesus' invitation to become like a child. Creative ways through and with our children, to reimagine our relationship with God.'
Alan Charter, Global Children's Forum

'Anna simply but profoundly unlocks many of the lessons we learn from the children in our lives, and how these lessons can deepen our relationship with our heavenly Father. A unique treasure of a book.'
Lucy Rycroft, The Hope-filled Family

'These thought-provoking, practical and relatable ideas will prompt even the busiest of parents to draw closer to God.'
Claire Burton, The Kitchen Table Project

15 The Chambers, Vineyard
Abingdon OX14 3FE
brf.org.uk

The **Parenting for Faith®** name and logo are registered
trade marks of Bible Reading Fellowship, a charity (233280)
and company limited by guarantee (301324), registered in
England and Wales

ISBN 978 1 80039 198 7
First published 2023
All rights reserved

Text by Anna Hawken 2023
This edition © Bible Reading Fellowship 2023
Cover image © digitalskillet1/stock.adobe.com

The author asserts the moral right to be identified as the author of this work

Acknowledgements
Unless otherwise acknowledged, scripture quotations are taken from The Holy Bible, New
International Version®, NIV®. Copyright © 1973, 1978, 1984, 2011 by Biblica, Inc.™ Used by
permission of Zondervan. All rights reserved worldwide.

Every effort has been made to trace and contact copyright owners for material used in this resource.
We apologise for any inadvertent omissions or errors, and would ask those concerned to contact us
so that full acknowledgement can be made in the future.

A catalogue record for this book is available from the British Library

BEING
GOD'S CHILD

A PARENT'S GUIDE

Ten things you can learn
from your kids

ANNA HAWKEN

CONTENTS

INTRODUCTION

If you have children in your life, it can feel like lots of your time and energy gets diverted into caring for them. You become known as somebody's mum, dad, step-mum or granny and can quickly find that this becomes your identity as well as your main focus. Many of us find it hard to start or deepen a relationship with God during a stage of life that can be emotionally and physically exhausting.

But it doesn't have to be that way.

Our kids and our relationship with them can actually help us grow to know God better. God describes himself as a parent – our parent. The Bible tells us that he is a 'father to the fatherless' (Psalm 68:5) and that he shows us compassion as a father shows compassion to his children (Psalm 103:13). So can we experience God like a child experiences him? Who better to learn from than the living, breathing examples already in our lives?

In this book, we will explore ideas to help discover what being God's child looks like for you. We'll take inspiration from the children in your life and your relationship with them. This is for all types of parents and carers, including step-parents, adoptive and foster parents, godparents, grandparents and other family members. You're not just a parent or carer; you can choose to be God's child too.

Every parent–child relationship is different. Your personal relationship with God and the way you understand him and interact with him will also be different from anyone else's. Part of being a child is the freedom to experiment and learn and grow. So this isn't a book for people who have everything figured out. It's for those of us who are open to trying and exploring ways to connect with him. It's about starting from wherever we are and working with whatever time and energy we have today. We may still have questions and struggles and lots else to juggle, but we want to see and understand more of God, our parent.

Don't worry about where you and God are at right now. Perhaps having a relationship with him is something you're considering or is new to you. Maybe you've known him for a long time but lots has changed since you became a parent (whether that was three days ago or 30 years ago). You might be going through an especially busy, joyful or complicated season where you're not quite sure how to relate to him. Wherever you're starting from today, let's explore these ideas and see what he shows us.

We'll look at all sorts of ways that our children and our relationship with them can teach us about how we can relate to God. It's not a perfect picture, but as something that we live and see and experience every day, it can help us to understand how God feels about us and what he is offering us. As your children approach and connect to you as a parent, you can do the same with God. Each time we interact with our children it can become a prompt to help us connect with God and a reminder to choose to include him in our day-to-day life.

Some ideas will strike a chord with you more than others, and that's fine. Have fun with them, experiment and enjoy the journey. These aren't tasks to complete, but inspiration for an adventure of getting to know your heavenly dad better. We will explore ten key ideas and each has some questions to consider. You can answer them on your own or chat about them with a partner, friend or small group of people. There are no right or wrong answers to these questions, they are just prompts to start you thinking. After that, there are some practical suggestions of things to help you connect to God as his child. How might your life look different if you were to really live this? Take it at your own pace. You may want to read this book slowly, exploring one idea a day, week or month, to give you time to try things out and find what might work for you.

The final sections of the book, 'Next steps' and 'Ideas to use with your children', explore how to help the children in your life connect to God and grow in their relationship as his child too. You can head there straight after reading each idea or focus first on figuring out what it looks like for you to be God's child, then come back later and explore it more with your children. Don't wait forever, though! You do not need to have it all figured out before you help your children go on this journey too: you can journey alongside each other. You will take different paths and go at different speeds, but you can help, support and guide them wherever you are. At points you may feel you're trailing behind them. That's great! Ask them questions and learn from them. When you have a breakthrough in your connection with God or your understanding of him, be willing to share that with them so they can learn from you too.

At the end of the book, there are notes for small groups to help you explore each idea more with other people.

I am on this journey with you. As a working mum of three, I am in the middle of learning to live as God's child in the busy day-to-day too. These ideas aren't just theory but come from my wrestling and experimenting with how to do that; from observing children, reading the Bible, asking God for help and talking to other parents and carers about what this looks like for them. I am so excited to see what God reveals to us as we explore these ideas. He is ready and waiting to show us new things about ourselves, about him and about our relationship with him. Let's start by exploring his offer and what that means.

THE OFFER

In the book of John in the Bible, in chapter one it says, 'To all who did receive him [Jesus], to those who believed in his name, he gave the right to become children of God' (John 1:12).

This is an invitation from God, to you, to become his child.

You can choose whether you want to accept that invitation or not. It is possible because of God's goodness and how much he loves us. He wanted a close parent–child relationship with us so much that he sent his Son to become a human on earth and to die in our place. This removed everything that was stopping us from coming close to God, and him to us. If we choose to accept him and everything he is and has done for us, we can have a parent–child relationship with him, now and forever.

It's not a one-off deal. Some people think choosing to be a Christian is a bit like when you sign up for a mailing list to get a freebie. You tick the box, take what's on offer and never think about it again. God is offering us much more than that. He's offering a relationship, not a transaction. A relationship with commitment on both sides. He offers to adopt us, giving us a permanent place in his family. Here we can experience love, care, acceptance and parent-child interaction throughout every day. If we accept that offer, we choose to be part of his family forever, through all the ups and downs. We are his children not only on the days when we feel like it, but every day. It becomes part of who we are. Knowing God loves us and is with us allows us to do and experience so much more than when we try to tackle life on our own. If you haven't said yes to that, is that something you want to do? If you're still on the fence, I'd encourage you to try thinking about and connecting with God in the ways this book suggests and take it from there. If you have accepted that offer, are you living your day-to-day life as his child? Or are there more ways you could connect with him and invite him to parent you?

As a child, you are known and loved. You can approach God and interact with him being sure of those things. You don't need to do anything to earn his approval or his love. It's a given. He knows everything about you. God declares this many times in the Bible as he speaks to Moses ('I know you by name' – Exodus 33:17), Jeremiah ('Before I formed you in the womb I knew you' – Jeremiah 1:5) and all of Israel ('I have summoned you by name; you are mine' – Isaiah 43:1). He knows things about us that even we couldn't know, like the number of hairs on our head. In John chapter 10, Jesus talks about being a good shepherd who knows his sheep (us) by name and that we know him and know his voice. There is nothing about you that he doesn't know, so you're not going to surprise or shock him. He is consistent and loving and constant. He promises never to leave us nor to forget us.

There are differences between human parent–child relationships and a relationship with God, two of which are important to highlight before we dive into the ten ideas we are going to explore together.

Firstly, God isn't like people. He is always loving and doesn't get things wrong. We can rely on him to be a perfect parent. This isn't true for us! None of us are perfect parents or have had perfect parents. Even if you had or have a great experience of being parented, they won't have got everything right. Even if you are a fantastic parent, you will have your off days. With every example and idea that we explore, keep that in mind. Images and illustrations help us understand, but they won't explain or mirror everything. Our view of God is shaped by many things. Our upbringing, our family, our friends and things we've watched, heard or experienced all play a part. Not all these ideas will be a true reflection of who God is. As you read, if something feels jarring or uncomfortable, pause. Ask if you're assuming God is like you are as a parent or how your parents or carers were to you, rather than the perfect parent that he is.

Secondly, if we want to be God's child, it is something that we choose. Our children didn't get a choice about arriving into our lives and our families. We gave birth to them, adopted or fostered them. In contrast, if we choose to be God's child, it's a decision we're making to be in a relationship with him. It's not something he forces upon us. He makes it available to us and lets us decide if it's something we want. It's not that he doesn't care. He wants us to choose a relationship with him, but the decision is ours. He wants children, not robots! This means if we choose to say yes to this offer, then we're giving him permission to parent us. We are asking for his help, love, guidance, correction and protection. In all the different ways that we're going to explore over the coming chapters, we are choosing to be in a relationship with him.

The great news about these differences is that it means we as parents don't need to compete with God. Our children need us, and they need God. God offers them things that we never could and has put us in their lives to be part of helping, loving and guiding them. We don't need to compare ourselves to God and judge our parenting based on that. He loves you and he loves them. He's here alongside you, a supportive and loving parent for you, as you parent them.

If you've read enough to take up or explore this offer, then let's look more at ten ideas of different ways that we can be like children with God...

SPEND TIME WITH HIM

When you become a parent, you soon discover there is not a lot that you do on your own anymore! Right from when they are born, our children are programmed to seek to be near us. They cry when they want to be fed or changed or held. As they grow up, they learn to say or show this: 'cuddle me', 'watch me', 'play with me' can be heard over and over again. They lift their arms up, dance around in front of us or start driving a toy car up our leg. They appear by our side or in our arms multiple times throughout the day and night. They are not worried about interrupting us, or what else we have to do. It doesn't matter if we were attempting a toilet trip in peace or trying to finish an email. They assume we are always there for them, that we are ready to respond to their needs, hear their thoughts and ideas, get excited about what they've done or just spend time with them. They delight in receiving our time and attention. Whether you have them full-time or not, when you are with them, their demands for attention can feel unrelenting. They always want to be with us, and they assume you want to be with them too!

There's a point to all this together time. It helps to keep our children safe and get them what they need. It's also essential for growing and strengthening their relationship with us. There is no shortcut or substitute. Every second, minute and hour spent together is valuable. Each one helps us understand, trust and know each other better. In his book *Outliers: The story of success* (Penguin, 2008), Malcolm Gladwell popularised 'the 10,000 hour rule' – that it takes 10,000 hours to master a complex skill, like playing a musical instrument. You don't wake up and discover you're great at something; you master something by investing time in it. Relationships are no different. It takes time to grow to understand someone. When they are first born or you first adopt or foster them, you and your child are strangers, who get to know each other better over time. We spend time with our children in all sorts of ways, including:

* Making memories together

* Having fun together

* Teaching them and trying new things with them

* Celebrating special occasions and achievements

* Doing routine and boring things

* Comforting and helping each other

Each of these experiences draws us closer together and makes our relationship stronger in different ways.

Sometimes we keep God for Christmas and crises, and we're missing out on so much if we do. When he invites us to be his children, he is offering to always be available for us to spend time with him. He wants to do all those different things with us because he loves the way that this grows and strengthens our relationship. He is never too busy. We can be sure that he is always with us, there for us to chat to and share whatever is going on in our lives. In the book of Jeremiah, God reminds his people that he is always near to them (Jeremiah 23:23–24). In Psalm 139, the writer describes how God is with us everywhere we go. He's there to have fun with and make memories with. He's alongside us as we learn or try new things. He sees and wants to join in celebrating our special occasions and achievements. He's there as we go about our usual routines and available to comfort and help us when we need it. As adults, though, we get busy. We get distracted by other things. We don't always realise or we forget that God's available and wants to be invited to do all those things with us.

Spending time with God doesn't need to be a pressure or another thing to fit in to our day. There are loads of little ways that we can spend time with him throughout our day and our week. I like to think of spending time with

God like drinking coffee (or Coke or a cuppa). There are different ways that we enjoy our favourite drink. If you already have a relationship with God, ask which of the below best describes how you most connect and spend time with him at the moment.

Routine

For many people it's part of their routine – they have a coffee when they first wake up or in a mid-morning break. It's something they're used to doing as part of their day. It can be helpful to have touch points like this with God. When you first wake up, when you go to work, when you're folding the washing, brushing your teeth or getting ready for bed. Pick a time (or times) and decide to tell God something. This could be anything about what you're thinking, feeling or doing. It could be something that's worrying or annoying you, something that made you laugh or something you're confused about. Anything at all. He wants to hear it all. You could ask him something; good communication is rarely one way. If there's not much to say, you can invite him to be a part of whatever you're doing. You can say these things in your head, whisper or say them out loud, or write them down in the notes on your phone or with an actual pen and paper. It's something we can do on our own and with other people.

Spontaneous

Then there's the coffee that we have to keep us going throughout the day. It's not linked to a particular routine or time of day; we just think, 'Oooh, I fancy a coffee right now,' and pause to make, buy or ask for one. We can do that with God too. When we're feeling tired, when we hit a problem or when the idea pops into our brains, let's interact with him.

Scheduled

Finally, there are the coffees that we plan in advance, where we set a time and a date either to be on our own or to meet with someone else. It's worth doing that with God too. Whilst it's great to check in with him in the middle of other things, sometimes intentionally setting aside a bit of time is what helps us to connect. Some people do this daily, and every morning or evening they read some of the Bible and/or share with God what's on their mind. Many parents find it difficult to get a regular chunk of time to do this each day. Opting for setting some time aside less often can make this more doable. Maybe you have some time whilst watching a child's swimming lesson, during nap time, or lying awake waiting to hear the front door so you know your teen is home. If you get the chance, you could go somewhere else for a change of scene. Experiment with what works for you in the stage of life you're in right now.

All three of these are good ways of enjoying coffee, and of connecting with God. It's not a case of one way being 'right'. God loves it when we choose to spend time with him. He's excited for however you want to choose to spend more time with him.

Questions to explore

1   Which of these three ways of connecting with God do you feel most drawn to? What do you think might work well for you in this season of life? If you already do one or two, how do you feel about trying the others out?

2   What are things that you enjoy doing? Do you invite God into them? Could you?

3   What are some things that you find difficult, tiring or draining? How is God a part of that? How could you share that with him?

Ideas of things to try

- Remind yourself to check in with God – sharing what you're thinking and feeling or asking him to be near to you. Some ways to regularly remind yourself are changing the lockscreen on your phone, or putting a sticky note by your bed or in your bag.

- Set aside time in your day, week and month to spend with God. Experiment with what works for you. Don't be disheartened if you don't find something that's a good fit for your life right now. If it's not working, try changing it.

- Practise telling God about something which others might find boring but that you really care about.

- Read a verse or short section of the Bible and ask God to make something stand out to you. You could start by reading the book of John or choose an app that sends you a verse a day or suggests a Bible reading plan. Share with God anything you especially like, don't understand or don't agree with.

- Try out one of the ways of connecting with God (connecting as part of a routine, spontaneously throughout the day or setting time aside) that you haven't tried much before.

- Next time you have a coffee (or Coke or builder's brew), tell God how you most like spending time with him. Use the smell or the process of buying or making a drink as a reminder to chat to him.

ASK LOTS OF QUESTIONS

What's the world record in your house for the number of questions a child has asked in one day? I'm pretty sure we've hit triple figures! Many kids go through stages where they have masses of questions. Each one seems to lead to another; it's like their curiosity is never satisfied. As they get older, they may not volunteer questions so readily. But given time and something to spark a conversation, they will have things they'd love to know the answer to or your view on.

Like it or not, Google and Alexa are never going to take over answering your child's questions! Because questions are about so much more than answers. They are a different and valuable way to connect, interact and learn about each other and the world. Asking them has loads of benefits for a child, a parent and their relationship.

1 **It helps children feel heard and understood.** It's powerful when a child asks questions and sees that a parent is listening to what they are saying. They learn that their thoughts and questions are valid and welcome, that what they think and what they have questions about is important. This makes them feel known and close to their parent. It encourages them to ask more.

2 **It helps parents learn more about their children.** As a parent, we can learn so much about our child by the questions they ask and when and how they ask them. We discover their interests and what they care about. It can reveal their current worries or challenges. It highlights areas where we could help them or communicate in a different way.

3   **It builds trust.** A child will put a parent's answers to the test, comparing the answer given with their own experience (past or future). If they find the parent is answering in a way that is reliable and helpful, they learn that their parent is a safe and good source of information. This encourages them to come to us for advice and guidance in the future.

4   **It helps us to understand each other better.** Our thoughts, feelings and views are all shared through exploring questions together. When a child asks, 'Why is Grandad ill?', they are not only asking for a factual answer. They may be interested in the name of the illness and how he developed it. They might also be asking why we think he is experiencing suffering, how we should respond or what might happen in the future. Our responses can include not only facts, but also our views and experiences. This could be what we think about some of those deeper questions and why. At other times, it might be the things we have seen or experienced that shape the way we respond to the question. This all helps our children know us better.

When we ask God questions, we can experience all these benefits as a child. We know he wants to hear what we have to say, and we can feel validated and understood as we ask them. He already knows everything about us but loves it when we share our heart with him. He invites us to ask him about whatever is on our mind. Through his responses, we learn more about God and the way he sees things. This can change us and the way we think about things too. It also builds our trust in him, when we find him to be a safe place and a reliable source of information.

We can see examples of this in the Bible, which records many different people's conversations with God.

One man called Habakkuk lived around 600BC. He was frustrated about injustice and kept asking God questions about why it was happening and what God was doing about it. God answered him by assuring him that he knew what was going on and would bring justice. Habakkuk came back with more questions and God responded again. This time, he asked Habakkuk to write down what he saw and heard as God explained. He not only answered Habakkuk's questions but told him other things to help him too. Habakkuk kept being honest about how he was feeling and what he saw. He asked God questions and waited for his response over and over again.

In a conversation with a man called Jeremiah, around a similar sort of time, God said, 'Call to me and I will answer you and tell you great and unsearchable things you do not know' (Jeremiah 33:3). This is an invitation for us too. When we choose to ask questions to God, he wants to share answers and insights with us.

The Bible also has poetry in it, much of which has people asking God questions. One of these poetry books, Psalms, has over 50 questions that people ask God. Many of them were written by a man called David. God describes him as a man after his own heart (1 Samuel 13:14), clearly someone who he likes spending time with. As David is honest and questions God, they connect with each other, and their relationship grows.

As we get older, we tend to stop asking so many questions. Why is that? Is it because we're busy and we don't take time to pause and think about what our questions are? Are we scared that we won't know the answer or won't like the answer? Have we stopped being curious about the world, God and relationships, and now just accept things the way they are?

What if we were brave and started asking more questions again? We've already seen this is an amazing way not only to learn but also to grow a relationship. You can ask questions about anything. About the big picture and the tiniest detail. About things that affect all of humanity and things that are personal only to you. You can ask God deep questions about life and death and suffering and things that aren't fair. You can ask him questions about the things that you care about – your family, your work, your health. We don't have to be polite and tone down our questions for God; he invites us to ask anything.

When you ask a question, pay attention to what God might communicate to you. It may not be in the way that you expect. In the Bible, we see some of the different ways that God communicates and answers questions. This might be through:

The Bible

As you read or listen to the Bible, you might find an answer to your question. It may be that a particular word or phrase stands out to you in a new way.

Words, pictures or ideas

Sometimes when we ask God a question, a word, a picture or idea can pop into our mind. We often won't know what it means straight away. Try asking God, 'Why have you shown me that?' or 'What does that mean?'. He may give you another word, idea or picture which helps you to make sense of it.

Other people

As they share their experience or something God has communicated to them.

Feelings

Sometimes we get a sense or a feeling that God is telling us something or feel a physical sensation in our body which helps us know his response.

Dreams

Sometimes the words or pictures in our dreams can be God showing us something.

However you ask your questions and whatever they are about, find a way to do it more, just like a child. Don't hold back. No topics are off limits, and he never gets tired of us asking 'Why?' Be open to the many different ways that God might respond and choose to connect with you through that.

Questions to explore:

1   Do you have any questions that you've always wanted to ask God but never have? What's stopping you from asking them?

2   Do you have questions about God that you want to explore? Do you have places you could do that? That might be talking to a Christian friend. It could be finding somewhere that you can ask questions, like an Alpha or Christianity Explored course.

Ideas of things to try:

• Every time a question comes to mind, ask it to God, there and then. Don't worry if you don't have time to stop and wait for an answer. Simply get used to asking God every time you have a question for him. You may be able to look back later and see how he has started to answer it, or ask the question again.

• If you don't have a lot of questions, reading the Bible can help you to have more. You can use an app or Bible reading plan. Don't worry about reading lots in one go; you can get questions just from a few sentences. Try asking God how he felt about different situations, why people did certain things or what a word or verse means. Looking in a study Bible or doing this with a friend might help you get answers to some of the more confusing sections. Some questions have no right answer; don't worry about that.

• Try asking God a question about yourself. Something like 'How do you see me?', 'What Bible verse do you want to share with me or remind me of?' or 'What do you want me to do today?' Grab a pen and paper and write it down. Be still and ask the question to God in your head. Write or draw any words, pictures, ideas, Bible verses, thoughts or feelings that pop into your mind or body. It may not seem related initially, but write it down without judging it. If you don't feel, see, hear or experience anything, don't worry. Try again another time or another place. You may want to do it with someone who is used to asking God questions and ask them to explain what they're doing and why. If you do see, hear or experience something, ask God to tell you more. Again, write down the explanation that comes to mind. Don't worry about judging and evaluating it, just write it down to begin with. When you have a moment, go back and see what you've written. See if it makes sense with what you know about God from the Bible. For example, the Bible tells us that God loves us. So if you felt he was saying something unloving, you can discard that thought. You can always ask someone who has more experience of listening to God to help you work out if it's from him and what it might mean.

- Next time your child asks you a question, use that as a prompt to ask God a question of your own.

MESS UP BUT DON'T GIVE UP

Have you ever met a child who didn't make a mess or make mistakes? It's not a thing! They all sometimes get things wrong, make poor choices or miss what they were aiming for. This is a natural and important part of their learning. Although they can find it frustrating, they don't give up on what they are trying to learn when they don't get it right the first time. Think about how many failures, false starts and mistakes happen as they get to grips with talking, getting their own breakfast, handling different social situations or learning to drive!

This is rarely a smooth journey, and as parents we are an important part of supporting them through the process. None of us feels like we always know the best way to do this, but we try to help them as they navigate it. Think about a child learning to walk. It requires lots of patience from you and them. You don't give up on them as a non-walker when they take a few shaky steps and fall on their bum. With great joy and excitement, you encourage them to get back up and have another go. You celebrate every teeny bit of progress they make in the right direction. When children are learning to walk, they need encouragement and time to practise. In a similar way, they need all kinds of support as they get older. When they fight with their siblings, they need an outside person to help them work out how to bring justice. When they make poor choices, they need boundaries and correction. When they have friendship struggles, they need empathy and help to decide what to do.

As adults, we make plenty of messes and mistakes too. They are not always as obvious as the ones we see our children make but we are still works in progress, like they are. However, when we mess up, we are not always as resilient as our children. We might not admit that we've made a mistake and try to bluff our way through and avoid the consequences of our actions. Other times we might over-focus on what has happened and write ourselves off as failures or beat ourselves up with the lie that we are a bad person. When we mess up, it draws our focus to ourselves. That can make us feel distant from

God – the very person we need to support and help us when we're struggling. Adam and Eve, the very first humans, did this in the garden of Eden. They walked closely with God until they made a mistake, then the guilt and shame from that led them to hide from him. That isn't what he wants for us.

As God's child, we have a parent who is perfect and committed to walking us through our failures and messes. God is a father who delights in us. He cheers us on and celebrates our progress. He expects there to be mess and mistakes as we grow, and those don't stop us from being his children. He says that there is nothing that can separate us from his love. There is nothing we cannot bring to him and be forgiven from and have him help us with. He always wants to restore our relationship with him. God is patient with us (2 Peter 3:9). He doesn't give up on us but wants us to come to him so that he can change our hearts and lives.

It's easy to assume that God the Father will respond to us the way our parents or carers did when we were kids. That might be with anger, punishment, pity, sarcasm, harsh words or denial of our feelings. That can make us fearful of approaching him with our struggles and mistakes, but we don't need to be. God the Father never does those things. He draws us close rather than pushing us away or putting anything between us. The Bible says he is 'compassionate and gracious, slow to anger, abounding in love' (Exodus 34:6). He wants to help us when we mess up to get up and carry on. If we need to say sorry and learn something, he can support us through that too.

Rachel Turner uses a picture that can help us understand what God wants for us. It's of a small girl sitting in a sandpit, eating sand:

> The sand is dirty and all over her face and mouth. Even though it's not good for her, and she's coughing and spluttering, she won't come out of the sandpit.
>
> Her father hates this. He's sad when he sees her there, particularly because he's built her a beautiful playground right next to the sandpit, with all sorts of things for her to climb on and enjoy, and he has a great big ice cream in his hand for her. So he goes over to her. 'Don't eat the sand!' he says to her. 'It's dirty and it's not good for you. Come out and I'll clean you up and we can play together and you can eat this ice cream.'
>
> But the little girl ignores her father. He tries again, telling her firmly that she needs to get out and play in the new playground. But she says, 'No.' Her father is so upset. He hates the sand because it is getting in

the way, stopping them being together. He's sad because she keeps choosing the sandpit, not all the lovely things he has for her, and he wants her to choose right.

Finally, the little girl gives up. She looks at her father and realises how sad he is, how much he loves her and wants to be with her, and what beautiful things he has made for them to do together. She decides she wants to get out of the dirty sandpit, and as soon as she lifts up her arms her dad beams at her as he swoops down to pick her up. He lifts her out of the mess and gently washes her so all the dirt is washed away. Now she is ready to play with her dad in their wonderful new playground.

Just like that father, God hates sin because it is bad for us and keeps us away from him. He loves us, and wants to be close to us. When we sin, like when the little girl ate the sand, he gets sad because he sees us choosing things that hurt us and take us away from him and stop us being close to him. When we realise we are sinning and say, 'I don't want this anymore,' God sweeps us up and cleans us up.

Reproduced from **parentingforfaith.org/post/sandpits-and-sin**

So how do we ask to get out of the sandpit? What happens when we realise we don't like where we are or what we've done and when we want to say sorry for the mess and ask for help to change? We ask God, our parent, to come and help us. We tell him we've messed up or we're in a mess, but we don't want to give up and stay there. How you do that is up to you! In Matthew 6, Jesus teaches his friends a prayer to show them how they can talk to God. It includes the lines 'Forgive us our sins as we forgive those who sin against us'. Think of that little girl in the sandpit. Sin is when we choose what we want. It's not God's best for us and it gets in the way of us being with him. Asking him to forgive your sins is like saying, 'Sorry, I'm ready to come out of the dirty sand now. Please come and make me clean again.' You might want to use the words from that prayer (you can find the Lord's Prayer in Matthew 6:9–13) or your own version of it as part of a daily or weekly rhythm or routine. You could also, in the moment, say in your head: 'Argh, I messed up. Sorry, God. Help me.' Other people like to have a time or space to pause and reflect. Some choose to write down what they want to say sorry for and move away from. Find what works for you.

Sometimes our children know when they've done something wrong and sometimes the parent has to point it out to them. This is similar in our relationship with God. Sometimes we know we've made choices that have taken us away from God and his best for us. When we realise this, we can go to him and say sorry and ask for his help to take us out of there. None of us gets things right all the time, and God encourages us to regularly come to him and ask for forgiveness and help. At other times, we may not have even realised our mistake, but as a loving parent God wants to draw our attention to what's happened and where we are. Like the father of the girl sitting in a dirty sandpit when there's a playground next door, God helps us see what's going on. This helps us learn and maybe choose differently next time too.

Two of the ways he does this are through the Bible and through the Holy Spirit. As we read the Bible, we get to know what God is like and which things he wants for us and which he doesn't. There are also lots of examples of people making mistakes, which show us what can cause problems for him, for us and for other people. If you're struggling with a particular issue, find out if the Bible has something to say about it.

In John 16:8, Jesus explains that he is going away but that he will send us a helper, called the Holy Spirit. The Holy Spirit can also highlight to us when we're doing, thinking or saying something that isn't good. This is not the same as feeling guilt or shame, which are not from God. It is the feeling we get when we see what we're doing, thinking or feeling from God's perspective. When what we're doing or thinking doesn't match up with God's way of doing things, we can experience a discomfort which can be a prompt to change something. It's like that moment of realising we're sitting in a dirty sandpit when we could be playing in the playground. If you feel like the Holy Spirit might be nudging you that something isn't quite right, ask him. As we saw in the last chapter, he might communicate to you in all sorts of different ways to help you work out where you are and what to do next.

This isn't about never getting anything wrong. You will mess up – you're human and you're a work in progress! But that doesn't mean you have to give up. You have a loving parent, ready to save you and take you to a better place as soon as you ask for his help and forgiveness. Doing that and knowing his love and acceptance is an amazing way to feel close and connected to him.

Questions to explore:

1 What reaction did you get from your parent(s) when you made mistakes? Are you assuming that is how God will respond to you too?

2 Do you make time and space to say sorry to God and ask him to help you? How? Where? If you find it tricky, what are the barriers that stop you?

3 Is there anything right now that you need to say sorry to God for?

4 What would help you to ask God to show you if there's anything you need to turn away from or make right with other people?

Ideas of things to try:

● Experiment with different ways of saying sorry and see what works best for you. It might be chatting to God about it as soon as you notice something's up. It might be using those little pauses in the day, whether that's a commute, a toilet trip or a car journey, to ask him. Or it might be making time or space daily or weekly to reflect and review what's been going on. You could use your own words; the words Jesus teaches his disciples in the Lord's prayer – 'Forgive us our sins as we forgive those who sin against us'; or the words that David uses in Psalm 51.

● Read the Bible verses mentioned in this chapter and the small group notes. If a verse stands out to you, learn it or put it somewhere you'll see it often as a reminder of God's forgiveness.

● If there is an area where you keep messing up, find one or two trusted friends and ask if you can meet or call them and share. Ask them to pray for and with you.

SHARE YOUR EMOTIONS

Children tend to be pretty good at showing and sharing their emotions, especially little ones! When they're happy, they beam. When they're sad, they cry. When they're angry, they punch something (or someone!) and throw themselves on the floor. When they feel something's not fair, they shout it at the top of their lungs. When they hurt themselves, they seek comfort from a parent or caregiver. It's clear to see what they are feeling. It looks different as they get older, but most tweens and teenagers also show and share their feelings. That might be through a slammed door, an angry text or giving us the silent treatment when they're feeling low. Or a hug, fist bump or happy GIF when they're feeling good.

This helps them and us to see what's going on inside them and what might need to happen about it. Imagine an emotion is like the warning light that appears on your car dashboard – it's an indicator of what's going on that you might not otherwise notice. It's a clue to the bigger picture. You can choose to ignore it, or you can choose to work out what that symbol means and take action. You might need to pump up a tyre or refill the oil. This helps keep the car working well and saves you problems further down the line.

As children show their emotions, it helps them and us to understand what they are feeling. This enables them to process what's going on under the surface. Expressing the emotion makes visible something that might otherwise go unchecked. It helps us spot opportunities to help them, encourage them or step in to sort a problem. As parents, we don't always know how to respond to their emotions, but based on what we can see, we try to help them work out what to do next or provide them with what they need. A child who is crying is showing they are sad and might need a hug and some kind words. A child who is smiling is showing they are happy and might need a parent to smile back or give them a high-five.

As we grow up, many of us learn to suppress or hide, or at least tone down, these outward signs. Some of us were told not to be so emotional or sensitive or not to cry. This encourages us to stop paying attention to those feelings. Over time, we become less adept at spotting them and knowing what to do with them. That doesn't mean they don't exist, though! One study found that people report experiencing an emotion 90% of the time.* Emotions are a huge part of our day-to-day human experience; there can be a tendency to assume that women are more emotional than men, but that same study found no significant differences between how often men and women reported experiencing emotions.

As adults, we can sometimes feel shame linked to the way we are feeling or that we are weak if we can't control our emotions. This can lead to us feeling isolated or confused. Sometimes those emotions pop up at a different time or get directed at a different person or thing. Have you ever had a reaction to something or someone that seemed out of proportion? Like when your child knocks something over and you shout at them, or someone asks if they can make you a cup of tea and you burst into tears. This can be a sign that we haven't acknowledged how we are feeling and talked to God or someone else about it. If we don't learn to recognise our emotions and share them, it can end up hurting us and the people around us too.

As a loving parent, God wants to be our safe place where we can express any emotion. In the Bible, God is described as someone who 'probes hearts and minds' or 'examines the thoughts and emotions' (Psalm 7:9). He doesn't simply care about what we do, he cares about what we're thinking and feeling too. The Bible also encourages us to 'Trust in him at all times, you people; pour out your hearts to him, for God is our refuge' (Psalm 62:8). Our human parents may not have always had a helpful or positive reaction to our true feelings. In contrast, God promises always to be a safe place to be honest about what we are thinking and feeling. In fact, he invites us to do this.

---

*Debra Trampe, Jordi Quoidbach and Maxime Taquet, 'Emotions in everyday life', *PloS ONE*, 10:12 (2015), available at **doi.org/10.1371%2Fjournal.pone.0145450**.

What if you don't know what you are feeling? For us as adults, that can often be the first challenge. We need to relearn to recognise our emotions. American psychologist Paul Ekman suggests that there are six basic emotions seen in all cultures – happiness, sadness, anger, fear, surprise and disgust.* Within each of those six, there can be many different variations and shades. We need to learn to notice when an emotion pops up and pause and ask what we are feeling. Is it any of those six? Is there a more specific word that helps us pinpoint what it is we're feeling? Sometimes having lists of words to choose from can be helpful. Search online for lists of emotion words and you will get plenty of examples. We can do this on our own or include God and ask him, 'God, what am I feeling right now?' Wait and see what he draws your attention to.

Recognising our emotions isn't the same as being a slave to them. Someone wise once told me, 'Emotions are like children: it's important to listen to them, but you don't need to do what they tell you!' We can worry that if we work out what we are feeling, then we are stuck doing whatever those emotions tell us. We think that if we can decide what we want to think and feel, then we will be more in control. Anyone who's tried that knows it doesn't work! It's impossible to choose what you feel. What you do have control over is what you do about that feeling. When we identify what we're feeling, it actually gives us more control to decide how to deal with it and what to do next. The Bible lists self-control as a 'fruit of the Spirit' (Galatians 5:22–23). This means that being able to control ourselves and make good decisions is a good thing which we can expect to see in our lives if we're living in a relationship with God. He can handle our emotions and help us as we decide what to do once we recognise what we are feeling. We don't need to be afraid.

Don't stop at asking God to help you work out what you're feeling. Take another step and choose to make a point of sharing your feelings with him too. How you do that is up to you – it might be in the moment or at the beginning or end of a day. It might be in your head or writing something down. God is here for us in the good, the bad and the ugly! It may feel very odd to you at first, but give it a go. Try sharing with him whatever you are thinking, feeling, experiencing and processing. He is always available and wants you to show and share your emotions with him.

---

*Paul Ekman, 'An argument for basic emotions', *Cognition and Emotion*, 6:3–4 (1992), pp. 169–200 and Paul Ekman, 'Are there basic emotions?', *Psychological Review*, 99:3 (1992), pp. 550–53.

If you don't like talking about emotions, well done for making it through this chapter. I know it's not within everyone's comfort zone! Be encouraged that this is for you too. You don't need to share your feelings with anyone except God and you don't have to do it out loud. I hope that helps. You can share knowing that you are always safe and accepted. You don't have to explain or justify yourself to him. He is an amazing confidant. For those of you who are comfortable sharing with other people, do that too. God puts other people in our lives to journey alongside us. In Paul's letter to the Romans, he says, 'Rejoice with those who rejoice; mourn with those who mourn. Live in harmony with one another' (Romans 12:15–16a). It feels good when people understand what you are feeling and meet you there, so seek out these opportunities to listen to and share with other people as well.

Emotions aren't the enemy! Practise recognising them, so that it is also clear with your children what you are feeling. Share them with God, who is always available for you and is a safe place to share whatever you are feeling. May that give you assurance of God's love and guidance, and use the insight it gives you to help you work out any next steps.

Questions to explore:

1 What are you feeling right now? You might want to use a list of emotion words to help you with this.

2 How good are you at recognising and sharing your emotions?

3 Which emotions have you experienced in the last week? Did you share them with God? Why, or why not?

4 What reaction did you get from your parent(s) when you showed and shared your emotions? Has that affected how comfortable you feel sharing them with God?

Ideas of things to try:

- Next time you notice an emotion, tell God about it. It can be as simple as saying (in your head or out loud) 'God, I feel…' If you have the time, you might want to tell him more about that. You could also ask him if he has anything to say back to you. Feel free to simply get used to doing the first bit and sharing what you're feeling with no agenda.

- Use your child's behaviour as a prompt for sharing your own emotions with God. If they scream, 'That's not fair!', tell God anything that you feel isn't fair in your life at the moment. If they're crying in disappointment about something, tell God what you're disappointed about. If they're excited about something coming up, tell God your hopes for the future and how you feel about them.

- Read a psalm and notice where the writer is sharing his emotions. Underline or highlight the ones that resonate with how you are feeling.

- Here are some suggestions of psalms to read if you are experiencing a particular emotion. Notice where the writer's emotions resonate with your own:
  - Angry at God – 44, 80, 137
  - Discouraged or hurt – 13, 22, 26, 42, 60, 69, 74, 79, 142
  - Frustrated about illness – 6, 38, 41, 88, 102
  - Grateful – 9, 18, 21, 30, 34, 40, 48, 66, 92, 107, 116, 118, 126, 138
  - Grieving or feeling loss – 6, 31, 77, 137
  - Hopeful – 2, 8, 16, 22, 26, 45, 69, 72, 89, 110, 118, 132
  - Hopeless – 5, 25, 27, 61, 143
  - Regret – 6, 32, 51, 106, 130
  - Struggling with temptation – 73, 141
  - Worried about someone else – 20, 72, 85, 115, 122, 128

- Try journalling or writing to God, sharing how you are feeling. You could keep a 'mood diary' by daily writing (on paper or on your phone) a word that best describes your emotions. Once a week or month, you could try sharing in more detail how you're doing. Try things out to see what most helps you feel connected to God.

ASK FOR HELP AND FOR WHAT YOU NEED

When you become a parent, you gain not one but hundreds of new job titles. You become a taxi driver, medic, sports coach, tutor, bespoke chef and master negotiator, to name a few. Our children expect that we'll have whatever they need, whether that's a plaster for a scraped knee, a song to lull them to sleep or a repair plan for the toy they've broken. They assume that we have the knowledge, skills, resources and love to help them. They are used to not being able to do things and asking for what they need. That might be a hand to hold to take some wobbly steps, a password to get into your Netflix account or a leg boost to get to the highest bit of the climbing frame. As we grow up, we can become more reluctant to ask for help and for what we need. We don't stop to think about what it is that we need. We don't know who to ask for help. We are embarrassed that we haven't worked it out ourselves, that we don't know how to do something or that we can't afford it. We don't need to be. We still have a heavenly parent who promises to give us what we need.

Throughout the Bible, God has hundreds of names, from Jehovah Rapha (our healer) to Jehovah Jireh (our provider). He's used to being called on for lots of things and needing to take on lots of different roles to be what we need. I remember God once showing me a picture to help me understand this. In this mental vision, I was toddler-sized and holding on to his adult-sized hand but weighed down by a humongous bag. He took it off me and we continued our adventure much more easily. As we went on further, it soon became clear that he had everything that I needed in his bag. Whatever the challenge or situation we met, he had exactly what I needed. Wellies, a raincoat and umbrella for the rain. Plasters, spare socks and new shoes for aching feet. A whole rope bridge to cross a giant gap. It got more and more ridiculous and Mary Poppins-esque! I began to understand the point. I can't think of, plan for and carry everything, and I don't need to. He has whatever I need.

As a parent, we often have to gather supplies for our children, carrying around the things they need in a change bag, a sports bag or the back of the car. We don't have to do that with other aspects of life! When we're focused on storing, collecting and carrying too much, it can distract us from focusing on the things that are important. We waste time and energy worrying when God has it in hand. Jesus told the crowds who were listening to him, 'Look at the birds of the air; they do not sow or reap or store away in barns, and yet your heavenly Father feeds them. Are you not much more valuable than they?' (Matthew 6:26). He used an example of something that people could see to remind them that God would look after them. Could your own children be this reminder for you? I know the endless requests for snacks or screen time can be draining. But, when they come and ask for something they need and you give it to them, remind yourself that you have a heavenly Father who wants to give you what you need too.

He invites us to ask him for what we need, instead of worrying. One reason for being cautious about doing that is because we are scared that he won't answer with what we want or in the way that we want and we'll be disappointed. Sometimes God does provide exactly what we need, exactly as we ask for it. However, he can also help us and grow us and our relationship with him through responding to our requests in different ways. In his letter to the Philippians, Paul writes to them, 'Do not be anxious about anything, but in every situation, by prayer and petition, with thanksgiving, present your requests to God. And the peace of God, which transcends all understanding, will guard your hearts and your minds in Christ Jesus' (Philippians 4:6-7). He doesn't promise that God will give them everything they ask for, but he does encourage them always to ask and to receive his peace. Psalm 37:4 says, 'Take delight in the Lord and he will give you the desires of your heart.' God isn't a vending machine that we go to, to get what we want. He is a wise, loving parent who invites us to come to him with whatever is on our hearts and minds. As we spend time with him and enjoy being with him, he can shape what it is that we long for and dream of. We become more like the people we hang out with, so over time this changes us. Without any extra work on our part, we begin to want what he wants for us and for the world, and he loves to give us those things.

There are many examples in the Bible of people asking God for help, and him sending it, albeit often in rather unexpected and unusual ways. In 1 Kings 17, we read some of the story of a man called Elijah. God asks him to go to a remote place and provides him with food delivered by ravens! This is a very weird delivery method, particularly for Elijah, as his religion considered ravens unclean animals. God loves to provide for what we need and often in ways that we don't expect. After this, Elijah goes and is part of God performing an amazing miracle to feed a widow and her son. Elijah was able to use his experience of God providing for him to help other people. I don't know about you, but I would feel nervous saying to someone on their last mouthful of food that God would provide, but this was straight after Elijah had seen and experienced God doing this for him. This gave him great confidence to ask God to provide for her. When we ask God for something and he provides it, it's not only for us. As we share what he's done or what he's given, it can also help other people ask and experience that provision too. When we share stories and examples of how God has provided for us, it gives other people boldness and confidence to ask God for what they need.

So, we've seen that asking God for help and for what we need isn't only about getting the thing or even only about us. It's also about our relationship with him. Every time we come to God and ask him for something, we show that we believe his promises and that we trust him. We communicate with him, which draws us closer. Each time we receive something from him, we are more confident to go back and ask again. God says that he loves to give good gifts to his children (Matthew 7:11). This brings him great joy and delight too! I was recently with a group of people where we tried asking God what to ask him for. One person felt God was saying, 'Don't go budget!' When we ask for big things from God, we show and affirm that he is powerful, that he loves us and that he wants to give us good things.

Is it possible that sometimes we don't ask because we don't know what we need and what we can ask for? We can ask God for anything. We can even ask him what to ask for! In Paul's letter to the Philippians, he tells them that 'God will meet all your needs according to the riches of his glory in Christ Jesus' (Philippians 4:19). God has an abundance of everything, and he can provide for all your different needs. You don't need to vet your requests for God. He wants to provide for you mentally, physically, emotionally and financially. Ask for patience, ask for friendships, for money, for wisdom about what to do next, for ideas about your parenting or work problems. In Idea 3, we talked about Jesus' example of how to pray, the Lord's Prayer (Matthew 6:9–13). In that prayer, he also teaches his friends to ask God for what they need, saying, 'Give us today our daily bread' (v. 11). He encourages them to focus on what they need in the here and now. Don't stress about the appointment next week or your three-year plan, but ask God for what you need for today.

I don't know your situation. You may be reading this with nothing left to feed your family, a destroyed relationship or a chronic health problem. I don't want to make light of any challenge you are facing. I don't claim that God is some kind of fairy godmother who will magically and instantly make it better. However, I do still think it's important that we ask. He tells us to. It's important for us and our relationship with him, for others and also to give him the opportunity to answer us, however he thinks is best. Throughout the Bible we see many examples of God providing people with what they need for the moment – not always what they want and not always in the way that they expect. He can provide through miracles or through other people. He can change priorities and perceptions. He can strengthen our relationship with him as we ask and trust him for what we need. Be bold and ask him for whatever you need for today. Be open to him answering in a way that you don't expect.

Questions to explore:

1   What do you need help with right now? What do you need?

2   Have you told God? Why, or why not?

3   What do you feel like his response is?

4   Do you believe God will give you what you need? Where have you seen him provide for you, people you know or people in the Bible? Where have you experienced disappointment or frustration in this area?

Ideas of things to try:

- Scribble down anything you've asked God for in the past where you feel he has provided for you or answered you. Thank him for those things and use it as an encouragement to continue asking God for what you need.

- When your child asks you for something, use it as a prompt to ask God for something. Don't stop and worry about whether now is a good time, just think of what you would like to ask God for right now, and do it!

- Ask God for what you need as you parent your children; that might be patience, sleep, or access to medical care. Tell him what's going on and what you need, whenever a need arises.

- Building on the ideas from the last chapter, next time you say, 'God, I feel...', add on 'and I need...'

- Write or type any Bible verses from this chapter or the small group notes that stand out to you. Use them as a reminder to ask God for what you need. Put them somewhere that you will see when you are likely to need something. That might be in your wallet or food cupboard or saving them as your phone lock screen. You could try to learn it rather than physically putting it somewhere.

✻ ✻ ✻ ✻ ✻ ✻ ✻ ✻ ✻ ✻ ✻ ✻ ✻ ✻ ✻ ✻ ✻ ✻ ✻

IDEA 6

APPRECIATE AND CELEBRATE

As a special treat, my husband and I decided to take our kids on an amazing adventure to a beautiful place with a light display. There were lots of areas, each with different music, stunning scenery and a breathtaking light show. We went all out, letting them stay up past their bedtime and drink hot chocolate in the woods. The next day their grandparents asked them about it. I thought they would overflow with excitement at all the amazing things they'd seen. 'It was brilliant... we went on a bus in the dark,' they said, referencing the short shuttle bus ride from the car park. It wasn't that they hadn't enjoyed the lights and music. They'd noticed and enjoyed *more* than the adults had. They were excited about a part of the experience we hadn't even thought to appreciate.

Children don't always see the world in the way that we do. They notice and appreciate all sorts of things that we miss as adults. They delight in little things as well as big ones, unusual things as well as those we'd expect them to enjoy. They slow down where we tend to rush on. We all know first birthdays are about enjoying the wrapping paper as much as the presents. As they get a bit older, they entrust us with the immense responsibility of looking after their prize possession – a special stick or stone that they have found and are completely amazed by. They are keen and excited to share everything they've received, made or achieved. Whether that's a new toy, a pee on the potty, a 'star of the week' certificate or getting to the next level of a game.

As they notice, enjoy and share, we teach them to sign, show or say thanks. It's all part of celebrating and appreciating those things. There are so many benefits to finding things to be grateful for and saying thank you for them. Research shows that, amongst other things, it protects us from stress, improves our physical and mental health, helps us to be resilient and improves our relationships.[*] We love it when they show or tell us that they are grateful. Of

---

*Giacomo Bono and Jason Sender, 'How gratitude connects humans to the best in themselves and in others', *Research in Human Development*, 15:3–4 (2018), pp. 224–237, available at **tandfonline.com/doi/abs/10.1080/15427609.2018.1499350**.

course, we don't do things for them or give them things to be thanked, but it's great to know that they are enjoying or appreciating something we've done for them, shown them, said to them or given them. We love them and we love to see them happy and enjoying what they've got or enjoying the world around them.

God loves it when we take the time to notice and enjoy all that he has given us, and he loves to hear our thanks too. He loves to see us appreciate the world around us and all that he's given us and does for us. As we grow up, we can lose our childlike sense of awe and wonder. We get used to our life, what we have and the world around us and stop noticing all that we've been given and get to be a part of. Often we are so busy juggling and managing all the responsibilities of adult life that we don't notice and appreciate what's right in front of us. When this happens, we can stop being so grateful.

So how can we slow down and rediscover how to celebrate and appreciate all that God has given us? Psychologist Robert Emmons suggests that there are two stages of gratitude.[*] The first is recognising there are things to be grateful for and the second is thanking the giver.

> ✳ Stage one: acknowledge that there are good things in your life
>
> To do this, we need to find ways to pause long enough to notice them. This is where we can learn from our children and the way they slow down to enjoy and appreciate things. It is easy to forget when we have busy lives and never-ending to-do lists, but it is important. Take a moment now to reflect on what might help you to do that in this season of your life. It might be a daily reminder on your phone or a gratitude journal or app. You could use your child's joy and wonder as a prompt. It might be as simple as getting into the habit of standing still, taking a deep breath and telling God something you notice that you're grateful for.

---

[*]Robert Emmons and Michael McCullough, 'Counting blessings versus burdens: An experimental investigation of gratitude and subjective well-being in daily life', *Journal of Personality and Social Psychology*, 84:2 (2003), pp. 377–389.

> ✴ Stage two: recognise you're not the source and say thanks
>
> As God's children, we need to go beyond feeling generally aware of things we are grateful for and acknowledge him as the giver by thanking him. That could be a quick thank you in our head, praying out loud or making time to write or take pictures of the things we are grateful to him for. Our decision to do that strengthens our relationship with him and the people around us. It's something we can join together in and agree on. When we say thanks to God, whatever is going on, it reaffirms that we believe he is good. When someone prays a prayer of thanks and you say, 'Amen', you're saying, 'I agree', or, 'We can agree on that.'

You do countless little things every day for your children. Filling out forms, preparing food, clearing up. Things they don't even see or notice. In a similar way, God is always working behind the scenes to help us, support us, guide us and encourage us. He gets things ready and sets things up for us. Deuteronomy 31:8 says, 'The Lord himself goes before you.' He's often putting in a lot of work behind the scenes that we don't see or notice. If you're stuck for what to thank God for, you could ask him about some of those things. Ask him to show you some of those little things he does so you can appreciate them. We love it when our children notice something we've done for them and say thank you. Can we do that more in our relationship with God?

As adults, we are also not as good at noticing our own achievements or we don't feel they are worthy of celebrating. As parents, we love to applaud and congratulate our children, even for little things. As our parent, God is proud of us too – whenever you get up to feed your baby in the night despite being desperate for sleep, whenever you support a friend in need, whenever you keep your temper in a tough situation. As a parent, you don't get many stickers, rounds of applause or bonuses. Much of what we do is unseen and uncelebrated by the rest of the world, but God sees it all. He is always available to celebrate and share our successes and achievements with us, even if we think other people might view them as small or insignificant. So don't be shy to share every success and triumph with him, whether it's huge or tiny. Ask him to highlight to you things you can be proud of to share and celebrate with him. He sees it all and he loves to affirm and encourage you.

The apostle Paul writes: 'Rejoice always, pray continually, give thanks in all circumstances; for this is God's will for you in Christ Jesus' (1 Thessalonians 5:16–18). He's reminding the Thessalonians, and us, that it's important to celebrate and enjoy all the good things that we see and experience. Then he encourages us to keep chatting to God and to thank him; to let thanks be part of our response to enjoying all those things. The 'in all circumstances' bit is important. This isn't about saying thank you on sunny days when everything is great. It's about recognising that, even in difficult circumstances, there are always things we can find to notice, enjoy and be grateful to him for. Sometimes the reason we don't celebrate and appreciate is that we feel life isn't going well for us. We're overwhelmed by the difficulties and challenges in our life, and we can't see anything to be grateful for. When we're struggling and in tough times, we can ask him to highlight what we can appreciate and celebrate. The Bible gives us some great examples of people turning to God with thanks and praise, even when things weren't going as they would have liked or hoped.

In 2 Chronicles 20, we read about a king called Jehoshaphat, who is in a difficult situation. Lots of other people groups have ganged up on him and his people and started a war with them. He chats to God and tells his men to go ahead of the army singing thanks and praise. He focuses on who God is and what they have to be grateful for, not the terrible situation they are in. He tells them to sing, 'Give thanks to the Lord, for his love endures forever' (2 Chronicles 20:21). They get to the place where they are expecting to find a vast army. Instead, they find dead bodies and lots of valuable equipment and clothing for them to take away. God had worked a miracle as they thanked and praised him! Choosing to celebrate and appreciate isn't a magic formula to get whatever you want. But this story does show the power of choosing to be grateful even in a difficult time.

There are two women in the Bible who find themselves having baby boys but under very different circumstances. Hannah, who lived around 1100BC, experiences the pain of infertility and cries out to God to give her a child. He does and she calls him Samuel, which means 'Because I asked the Lord for him' (1 Samuel 1:20). Even his name shows that she acknowledges that it was God that made it possible for her to have him. In 1 Samuel 2:1–10, we read her prayer of praise and thanks to God as she celebrates and appreciates Samuel's life. Over a thousand years later, Mary finds herself pregnant, despite being a virgin. Unlike Hannah, who longed and asked for a child, Mary's pregnancy was completely unexpected and put her in a very difficult position.

Like Hannah, she chooses to thank and praise God. She trusts him and his plans and purposes, even when that makes things complicated for her. Of course, it is a huge honour to be chosen to carry God's son, but it would be understandable if her focus was on the disruption, inconvenience and fear that would have come with this. We find ourselves in all sorts of situations in life. These women show us that the choice to celebrate and appreciate isn't just about our circumstances. Whether or not life is going the way we want, there is still always an opportunity to choose to see the good that is going on and thank God for it.

In Idea 1, we explored ways to spend time with God. Celebrating and appreciating the little things and thanking him for them is another great way to do that, which we can learn from our children. Some of us find it natural and easy to be grateful. Some of us find it much harder. Sometimes our circumstances make it more of a challenge to see what we can celebrate and appreciate. Wherever you are today, start small. Is there a tiny change you could make to the way you think or the way you do things that might help you to celebrate and appreciate more? Small changes can make a big difference. Thankfulness and celebration are good for us and a great way to connect with God.

Questions to explore:

1 What have you noticed recently that you were grateful for? Did you celebrate and appreciate that with God? How might you be able to?

2 What helps you to slow down and notice little things to be grateful for? What might work for you at this stage of life?

3 Are there difficult things in your life at the moment which make it hard to find things to be grateful for?

Ideas of things to try:

- Try a daily gratitude practice. This could be thinking of something as you brush your teeth, writing it in a journal or keeping a note on your phone. Gratitude apps like Gratitude and Presently can help you to do this.

- Any time your child thanks you, use that as a prompt to thank God too.

- As you go about your day doing things for your children, ask God to show you some of the things he does for you. Take a moment to thank him.

- When you're facing something difficult, whether that's a big life issue or cranky children at the end of the day, stand still, take a deep breath and ask God to help you notice something to be grateful for.

- Tell God something that you're proud of. Show him something you've made or tell him about something you worked hard at.

LET HIM LOVE, COMFORT AND PROTECT YOU

'Mum-eeeeee.' 'Dad-eeeeeeeee.' Go to any park, playground or public place and it won't be long until you hear these shouts. You probably hear them in the middle of the night in your own house too. A stomach bug, a bad dream or a misplaced special teddy all get our children calling for us. Wherever they are, children call out to their parent or caregiver for love, comfort and protection – when they're scared, when they're hurt, when they're lost or when they just want a reminder that we are there. It's not uncommon in our house to hear sobs of 'I want my mummy' even when I'm right there already holding them. It's their default cry when they need reassurance and comfort.

To thrive and flourish, all humans need emotional connections as well as their physical needs met. Ideally, they learn this by forming a secure attachment with a parent or primary caregiver as a baby. A strong emotional bond forms as a parent responds to their child's needs (Bowlby's Attachment Theory, 1969). This helps the child to feel secure and understood. It provides a safe base for them that helps them as they grow up and navigate the rest of the world. It enables them to connect to other people and have the confidence to explore and learn new things. As children grow up, their parents learn different ways to help them feel loved, safe and secure. They might need hugs, routine, a special soft toy, space, boundaries, music, good communication or something completely different. Each child is unique, and a parent or caregiver is the person who best understands them and what they need to help them feel loved and secure.

Not everyone will have experienced this in their childhood, or feel confident to know how to provide this for their children. We don't need to let that stop us from receiving the amazing gifts of love, comfort and protection from God. We can always be confident that he is available to meet our every need (Isaiah 58:11). He is a trustworthy and safe place to form a secure attachment. We can be sure that he loves us (Romans 8:37–39), his character will never change (Hebrews 13:8) and he will always be there (Joshua 1:5). This secure attachment can provide us with comfort and safety. It also helps us to understand how to build healthy relationships with other people. It gives us confidence to explore the rest of the world.

As we become adults, we can stop calling out for that love, comfort and protection. We get used to relying on ourselves and try to be self-sufficient. Sometimes we see it as weak to come to God and ask for those things, or we don't realise that we need his love, comfort and protection. Even as adults, we still need those things, so we will always go looking for them somewhere. If we don't go to God for them, we can seek them in places that are poor substitutes for God's pure, selfless version of them. It might be in other relationships. It could be by relying on our finances or achievements for security. Many people go to something like alcohol, caffeine, porn or online shopping for comfort when they are feeling low.

Let's look more at God's offer. When we understand what he wants to give us, it makes it easier to come to him. We don't need to be self-sufficient or look for it in other places. Psalm 91 is a great example of someone reaching out to God for his love, comfort and protection. There's no title, so the author is unknown, but some of the themes and phrases make it likely that it was Moses or David. It gives three different pictures, which are different ways of understanding who God is and the way he loves, comforts and protects us:

1 God as a refuge and a fortress – a safe place like a castle where you can hide and know his protection.
2 God as a mother bird – sheltering young chicks under her wings (see also Psalm 61:4).
3 God's faithfulness as a shield – he covers and protects us so that we can know we are safe.

Are any of these good pictures of how you experience or understand God?

The writer goes on to describe how this means you don't need to feel afraid at any time of day or night. The world and the people in it are a very different place if you can be sure of the love, comfort and protection of an attentive and available parent. It gives you the freedom to explore and adventure in the world without fear holding you back. God wants to be your safe place and comforter so that you have that freedom.

If our own parents were unable to protect us or chose not to, we might assume that of God too. This can become another reason that we don't call out to him, but God promises to protect us (2 Thessalonians 3:3). Have you ever seen a parent go into a different mode when their child gets bullied, injured or picked on? I have seen the most docile, placid parents turn into fierce warriors when their child gets thumped at soft play or sent offensive texts, storming the school gates or confronting the parent or child involved, swooping in to protect and resolve the situation. This is a powerful picture of what God wants to do for us. We see throughout the Bible that he stands for justice and fairness (Deuteronomy 32:4). God does not like people messing with his children! So often, love, comfort and protection are interwoven. God's not the sort of parent who stands at a distance and says, 'There, there.' He is powerful and ready to get involved. He offers us his strength and his help when we need it most. Knowing that provides a secure base for us to form relationships and to face all situations and circumstances.

Another possible reason we don't ask God for his love, comfort and protection is that we fear he won't respond how we hope and we'll feel disappointed or abandoned. One of my most challenging experiences was a difficult pregnancy and a baby who was born very tiny and ill. As a way of connecting with God, I asked friends and family to ask God for a song to share with me. When I was too exhausted and emotional to pray, I could play these songs. It was a way to feel surrounded by their truth and also the prayers of the people who had sent them. It helped me become aware of his love, comfort and protection when I felt very low. One that I particularly remember is 'Another in the Fire' by Hillsong United. It references both the biblical story of Daniel's friends, who worshipped God when it was forbidden and were thrown into a fiery furnace (Daniel 3) and the story of Moses and the Israelites crossing the Red Sea (Exodus 14). In both those stories, the men involved faced an impossible and horrendous situation, certain death! Daniel's friends from fire and Moses from the Red Sea and the Egyptian army. God showed his love and provided comfort and protection for them in different ways. Both were miraculous. For Daniel's friends, they remained in that fiery furnace, but God protected them there. (At another time, God sent angels to shut the mouths of the lions when Daniel had been thrown into their den. He came right alongside him. Daniel remained in the difficult situation but he wasn't harmed – see Daniel 6.) For Moses, he removed the obstacle. God told him what to do and the sea was parted to make a way, even when there seemed to be no way out. All these show God's amazing love, comfort and protection.

Think of a boat on a stormy sea. You're the boat, and the sea is whatever challenging situation you are facing. Sometimes God calms the storm. We know he can do this because we see him doing exactly that in Mark 4:35–41. He intervenes and changes things. This could be through a miracle, medicine, other people or changed circumstances. The situation is resolved, and all is well again. At other times, he lets the storm rage. As it does, he reminds us of his presence and protection, calming us and loving us, right in the midst of the chaos. Both are amazing. Given the choice, most of us would probably opt for the storm to stop. Yet I can tell you from experience, there is nothing that helps you understand God's love for you better than letting him be with you as the storm rages. You may not get to choose, but ask him for his love, comfort and protection, and watch for him to respond in either way.

Questions to explore:

1 Did you experience love, comfort and protection from your parent(s) or caregiver(s) when you were a child? Do you think this affects the way you view God offering this to you?

2 Do you feel like you ask God for his love, comfort and protection? If you find this difficult, what stops you or holds you back? If you find it difficult but aren't sure why, try asking God to bring to mind anything that is stopping you.

3 Are there places, activities or Bible verses that remind and reassure you of God's love, comfort and protection?

Ideas of things to try:

- Think back to a time where you knew God's love, comfort or protection. Thank him for it and ask him to keep covering you with that in the future.

- Next time you feel ill, overwhelmed or in danger, ask God to come close and parent you. Be honest about how horrible it feels and how fed up or scared you are. Ask him to help make you aware of his presence.

- When your child calls out for you to come close, ask God to do the same for you.

- Have a read through these verses and choose one or two to learn or put somewhere you'll see them. Remind yourself of them when you're facing something difficult.

'But the Lord is faithful, and he will strengthen you and protect you from the evil one' (2 Thessalonians 3:3).

'Be strong and courageous. Do not be afraid or terrified because of them, for the Lord your God goes with you; he will never leave you nor forsake you' (Deuteronomy 31:6).

'So do not fear, for I am with you; do not be dismayed, for I am your God. I will strengthen you and help you; I will uphold you with my righteous right hand' (Isaiah 41:10).

'God is our refuge and strength, an ever-present help in trouble' (Psalm 46:1).

- Read and reflect on Psalm 23, 91 or 121. What stands out to you?

- Listen to some music which helps you reflect on God's love, comfort and protection. You could start with 'Another in the Fire' by Hillsong United.

- With children who are upset, I like to use the question 'Are your feelings or your body hurt?' It's helpful because it gives them an opportunity to express any physical or emotional pain. It invites them to share their experience rather than have me assume what the problem is. You might find it helpful to imagine God asking you this question. What is your response?

LEARN FROM HIM

Have you ever heard a word or phrase come out of your child's mouth and realised that's exactly what you say? Or seen your child do something in a specific way and realised they are copying the way your partner does it? Children don't arrive in the world knowing everything they need to know. They have some basic instincts to help them survive, but for everything else they have to learn from the people and environment around them. We see them learning and growing all the time. The child who couldn't write their name a few months ago has finished a story. The tween who always wore the same T-shirt now has an ultra-cool fashion sense. The teenager who used to trip over their sentences now has a part in the school play. As their parents, they look to us to help them learn. This happens in lots of different ways. We guide them by teaching them ourselves and by directing them to places and people where they can learn more. Sometimes we deliberately teach them, showing or explaining how to do something. Other times it is more subtle. They copy phrases, behaviours and routines that they see us doing as they spend time with us. As we explored in Idea 3, it's a journey and they won't always learn what we want them to right away.

As adults, it's easy for us to become content with what we already know and our way of doing things or seeing the world. We stick to our own opinion rather than making time to learn from God and ask his view. Have you ever had a standoff with your child when you were trying to help them, but they thought they knew best? Imagine, for example, they try to stick a fork in the toaster. To you, the adult, it is completely clear why this is a bad idea. You have information and experience that they don't have. You know that you need to turn the toaster off at the socket and use the lever to get the toast out. But they think you're mad. To them it's obvious the toast is stuck, so they need to shove something in to get it out. Their reliance on doing it their way stops them from learning a better way. We can be like that with God sometimes. We see things from our angle and with our level of knowledge and experience and think we know what we are doing. Part of being his child is admitting we don't know everything. Choosing to keep learning from him and to trust that he has the big picture and the whole view when we don't. He sees and knows things that we can't (Isaiah 55:8–9). That's why we need to keep going to him and asking him to teach us more.

As our parent, God wants us to keep learning from him and the places and people he directs us to. We might not like to think of ourselves as still having a lot to learn or actively learning in our daily life, but we do. As well as bits of intentional learning, like taking time to read the news or watch a YouTube tutorial, we also learn and pick up lots from the environment around us. We learn from the TV we watch or the social media we browse about other people's lives and the way they do things. We watch people in the park and on the school run to see what they do. We ask our friends and family about their views. This all gives us information that affects what we think and feel about things and how we choose to live. This can be a real mixed bag. Some of it is helpful and some of it really isn't! We get some useful facts and good ideas, but it can also lead to anxiety, self-doubt or confusion. When we learn from God and the Bible, we know we are always getting good information. It's from someone who cares for us and wants what is best for us. It can provide balance and help us make sense of the information that we get bombarded with from other places. God is wise and trustworthy. He can help us with everything we need to know.

So how can we learn from God and from people and places that are good for us? Here are four different ways:

* Learning from the Bible

* Learning from spending time with God and talking to him

* Learning from other Christians

* Learning by teaching others

In different seasons of your life you may rely on one or two more than the others. But they're all useful ways of learning and growing, so don't throw one out without experimenting with it first. As we explore them, you might like to think about which ones you tend to rely on and which are less familiar to you.

Learning from the Bible

The Bible is full of all kinds of things we can learn from. In 2 Timothy 3:16 it says, 'All scripture is God-breathed and is useful for teaching, rebuking, correcting and training in righteousness.' It is full of God's inspiration and useful for all sorts of different things. The history books, like Joshua and Judges, give us loads of examples of things to do and not do. They give us the context and background information for where we are now. The wisdom literature, like Proverbs and Ecclesiastes, gives lots of good advice on how to live. The stories about Jesus that we read in the books of Matthew, Mark, Luke and John help us get to know what he was like. The stories he told often help us understand something about the way we should live. The letters, like Romans and Galatians, address all sorts of issues that the early church was facing, many of which we still face today.

The different parts of the Bible nourish us in different ways, so it's helpful to try to read or listen to a mixture. This gives us a more helpful and balanced view than always going to the same books or verses. Many of us know the Bible is useful but struggle to get motivated or find time to read it. With some creativity we can all find five minutes or more to make the most of this amazing source of wisdom. It might be listening to it in the car, whilst washing up or walking the dog. It could be using a Bible reading app – either with a plan, like YouVersion, or a more reflective one, like Lectio365. If you like going deeper, The Bible Project has some videos that help you get to grips with what's happening. Listening to a podcast series of Bible studies might be more your thing. We can also learn loads by reading the Bible with our children and letting them be part of challenging us and asking questions. Depending on their age and stage, you might want to use a children's version or simple text version. Change it up to keep it interesting. Many busy parents find little-and-often is more manageable than trying to tackle big chunks in one go.

Learning from spending time with God and talking to him

Paul writes to the Ephesians, 'Follow God's example, therefore, as dearly loved children' (Ephesians 5:1). Just as our children learn by copying us, we can learn by copying God. He is the perfect example for us to learn from. When Jesus was on earth he said, 'I only do what I see my Father doing' (John 5:19, paraphrased) and, 'My teaching is not my own. It comes from the one who sent me' (John 7:16). He learnt through constant communication with God, and we can do the same. Try asking God a question, such as 'What do you want to teach me today?', 'Is there anything new you want to show me today?' or 'How could I do this differently?' Be ready to notice any way that he responds. We looked at some of the different ways he might respond in Idea 2, if you want to revisit that. It could be a thought, a feeling, a dream, a Bible verse, words from someone else or an example or opportunity that he brings into your life. Children learn most from spending time with us and watching and copying what we do. (It's why 'Do as I say, not as I do' doesn't work!) The more time we spend with God, the more we find out about him. We become more tuned in to how he thinks and feels about things. This all helps us learn about how to become more like him.

Learning from other Christians

In Paul's letter to the Philippians he advises them, 'Whatever you have learned or received or heard from me, or seen in me – put it into practice' (Philippians 4:9). People learn by what they hear, but also by what they see. That's very obvious in our children as we see them copy us, but we can also copy other people. Do you have other Christians in your life that you can learn from? This could be one or two trusted friends, a small group, chatting to people at church or to friends and family. I've learnt so much about my relationship with God by pinching ideas from other people! Watch what other people do. Copy them or ask them how they handle different questions and issues. Keep in mind, however, that people aren't perfect! You need to strike a balance of getting ideas from different people that you trust. Be discerning about what to learn and who to learn it from.

Learning by teaching others

Teaching others something you have learned is an effective way of learning yourself. It's also a way to put into practice what you've learned from the Bible, from spending time with God and from other Christians. The Feynman

Technique suggests that when you're trying to learn a new skill, you write about the topic as if you were teaching someone else. Trying to explain something complicated using simple language helps you to work out what you know and what you don't. This is another perk of being a parent – you have people to try this out on! Don't worry about giving it a go, even when you're not feeling confident about what you know. The very act of teaching them will help you work out what you do know or think and where any gaps in your knowledge are. When you teach your children about God or the Bible, it's not only for their benefit. It's helping you in your learning and exploration too, so make time for it. It doesn't need to be a sit-down study time. Try sharing something with them whilst you're doing your normal daily activities. Share something new you've learnt. Share something that you found confusing and did some more research on or chatted to a friend about. Tell them where you're up to with it now, even if you haven't reached a conclusion.

Questions to explore:

1   How do you like to learn?

2   Who or what do you learn most from? Does this help you?

3   What have you learnt recently? About life in general? About God and the Bible?

Ideas of things to try:

- Try reading or listening to the Bible in some ways that you haven't tried before. A few hours later, come back and see what you remember. Decide which way you learn best.

- Read Psalm 32:8. Tell God that you want his instruction and counsel and ask him what he wants to show you today.

- Pick a question like 'What do you want to teach me today?', 'Is there anything new you want to show me today?' or 'How could I do this differently?' Ask that same question to God every day for a week. Write down what you think he is saying. Look back at the end of the week for any themes or anything that's changed in your thinking.

- Ask another Christian what they've learnt from or about God recently. Join a small group or arrange to have a coffee or a pint with a friend. If that's not possible, ping a few people a quick message or voice note and see what responses you get.

- Have a go at explaining something that you've learnt to your child or a friend (or a pet or plant if you're feeling really unsure!) You may have to try explaining it in different ways. Invite them to ask questions. Be honest if you don't know how to respond. It's fine to say, 'I'm not sure.'

JOIN IN WITH WHAT HE'S DOING

Part of being a child is that you go along with your parent and join in with whatever they are doing. What that looks like depends on the parent's interests and their work. My mum was a teacher, and I remember many mornings helping her set up the classroom. My dad loves writing songs and sketches, and as kids we would often get called upon to help him test or perform them. When you were a child, how did you join in with your parent or carer? As children get older, we may give them more choices about how they spend their time. But there are still times when we expect them to come with us and join in with our plans or help us with what we're doing. Part of being a child is looking at where you've been taken and what everyone else is doing and finding a way to get involved. If the family's gone to the beach and a child sees everyone else grabbing buckets and spades and starting to build a sandcastle, they are likely to do the same. They might do exactly the same as someone else or find their own niche designing, digging or collecting shells for decoration. Some of these things children join in with are just for fun, but others are about making a difference to the world and the people in it.

Every day, our parent, God, is working to transform the world. Part of being his child is joining in with him to help him change it. The Bible tells the big story of his activity in the world. In it we see his relationship with individuals and how some of them choose to join in with this important work. In the world we live in there are people who are hungry, lonely, afraid and struggling with all kinds of other issues. There are people who don't know God and the amazing offer of being his child and living in a relationship with him. God doesn't want it to be like this. He wants everyone to have what they need and asks us to be a part of making that happen. There are so many different ways to get involved with this. The way you join in will depend on who you are and where you are. We all have different things to offer and different ways to contribute. We don't need to have all the knowledge and skills, just to play our part.

My husband, Matt, is a musician and so being surrounded by music is part of our family life. One day, he was playing the piano with our eight-month-old on his knee. She started whacking the keys. His face lit up. 'Look at this, we're doing a duet!' he beamed. Whichever note she played, he worked it into what he was doing to make it sound good. God showed me that's a picture of what joining in with him is like. He is the master pianist with a beautiful and complex plan, but he loves it when we join him in that. It doesn't matter that our part can feel as unskilled as bashing notes. He's doing all the hard work of harmonising, chord progressions and linking it together. We are working on something and making something beautiful together.

It can feel overwhelming. There is so much need in the world, how do we know where to start? Which part of what God's doing do we join in with? I'd encourage you to start somewhere, anywhere! If we wait around for the perfect opportunity or for a specific instruction, we may never get going. I admire the way children can look at a sea of art supplies or construction toys and get going straight away. They don't have the hesitancy about how to begin that we sometimes struggle with as adults. Let's learn from them and get stuck straight in.

How do we do that? We see in the Bible that God is always looking after and championing the last, the least and the lost. He is always finding ways to give people what they need – food, water, shelter, safety and a relationship with him. Matthew 25:35–40 gives some practical examples. Jesus is telling a story and says, 'For I was hungry and you gave me something to eat, I was thirsty and you gave me something to drink, I was a stranger and you invited me in, I needed clothes and you clothed me, I was ill and you looked after me, I was in prison and you came to visit me… whatever you did for one of the least of these brothers and sisters of mine, you did for me.' Whenever we help people in need, we are joining in with what God is doing. There are hundreds of different ways to do that. It might involve standing up for justice, praying for others, being generous, campaigning for change, sharing about God with others and many other things.

What are the needs in your community? Could you help an individual – a friend, neighbour or someone else you know who is struggling? What about a group of people – a school, care home or toddler group? You might want to look beyond the local too. Is there an area of need that you feel strongly about? It might be an issue that you have personal experience of. Or it could be that you hear a story or news report that moves you. Joining in with what

God is doing can involve campaigning or working behind the scenes. Think outside the box and ask God to guide you and help you spot opportunities.

You might also want to start seeking out some more specifics about how God wants to use your unique skills, interests and talents. Take some time to ask him. Write or ask, 'God, how can I join in with what you are doing?' and write down whatever he brings to your mind. Look out for opportunities that he might highlight to you over the coming days and weeks too. If you don't feel you get a specific response, don't worry. Keep going with other ways that you are getting involved and be open to what else he might want to show you.

We live busy lives and it's easy to feel that we have too much already going on to join in with what God's doing too. As human beings we tend to focus first on our own wants, needs, desires and plans. The Lord's Prayer (Matthew 6:9–13) can be a helpful way of shifting our focus so that our own health and happiness isn't always top of the list. It's the model prayer that Jesus gave when his friends asked him how to pray. It starts by asking for God's name to be kept holy and his kingdom to come here on earth. After that it goes on to address our needs and sin and protection. But it begins with God's priorities and asking for him to continue his work of transforming the world. Praying this, or your own version of it, can help get those things back in the right order. It will always be tempting to choose our own comfort first, but Jesus is clear that his Father's work involves spending time with and helping people who aren't popular or pleasant. Jesus says, 'It is not the healthy who need a doctor, but those who are ill. I have not come to call the righteous, but sinners to repentance' (Luke 5:31–32). The thought of 'getting your hands dirty' can be scary, but it's so worth it! There's no joy in sitting on the sidelines. It's so much more exciting to get stuck in and find out what it's like to be fully involved.

Some of us go the other way and can try to get involved with everything and everyone. There will always be more needs than you are able to help with. Don't be put off by this. We're joining in with God's work of transforming the world. He doesn't ask or expect us to do it all. If you find yourself burdened and exhausted by it, chat to him about that. Ask if you need to step back from some things and leave them to other people. It can also be helpful to remember that we don't need to do anything to earn his favour. Think back to that example of the baby playing the piano on her dad's knee. The dad wasn't making music with the baby because she was the world's greatest pianist. God doesn't partner with us because we are superheroes. He chooses to invite us to work with him because we are his children and he loves us. We belong with him, and we don't have to do anything to fit in or to gain acceptance. We join in with what he's doing not to get brownie points but to enjoy doing something together and being part of his amazing plans.

Questions to explore:

1   What does God like doing that you like joining in with?

2   Where are you already joining in with what God is doing?

3   Does anything stop you or hold you back? What would help you overcome that?

Ideas of things to try:

- Ask him, 'God, what are you doing that I can join in with?'

- Next time you're doing something where you feel really alive, pause and ask, 'Where is God in this?' 'Is this part of what he's called me to do?' Thank him for putting you there or opening up that opportunity.

- Get involved with a charity, initiative or project in your local area. Is there something that helps some of the people talked about in Matthew 25 (hungry, thirsty, homeless, strangers, sick or in prison)?

- Ask other people how they join in with what God is doing. If something interests you, ask if you can try doing it with them.

USE THE FAMILY NAME

Imagine what it would be like to grow up as the child of someone rich and famous, as royalty or as the child of a celebrity. There would be a lot of perks! Not because of anything you've done but because of who your parents were. The family that you were born or adopted into would completely change your experience of life. You'd get the best seats and opportunities available. You would get exclusive access backstage or behind the scenes anywhere that you wanted to go. When people recognised your name, you'd get doors opened for you and you'd be rushed to the front of queues. Anything you needed would be brought to you and given to you. You'd have status, authority and unlimited resources.

That's a bit like what is available to us as God's children when we are adopted into his family. God is described as the 'King of kings and Lord of lords' (1 Timothy 6:15). Nobody is more powerful and has more authority than him. Jesus' name is the most powerful name there is. There is no name higher than his name and every knee should bow when they hear it (Philippians 2:9–10). As his child, you are personally connected to him. Jesus explains that 'whoever believes in me will do the works I have been doing, and they will do even greater things than these… you may ask me for anything in my name, and I will do it' (John 14:12, 14). Asking in Jesus' name is crucial to seeing amazing things. He invites us to use it.

He also gives us access to all his resources to help us do this. When you're in your parent's house, you probably have freedom and permission to raid the fridge or cupboards. You are not like a guest who may not feel it appropriate to take or use what's there. God gives us access to all that he has to enable us to keep doing his work. He says that as his children, we inherit all that he has. The apostle Paul says, 'Now if we are children, then we are heirs – heirs of God and co-heirs with Christ' (Romans 8:17). As his adopted children we get to inherit all that he has to give us, the same as Jesus does. This is for now, to enjoy here, in this life, and for the next, where we get to be with God too.

Heaven is a place with no pain and suffering that we can look forward to enjoying. One day, God is going to make everything new. He is going to bring heaven and all the amazing things about it to earth (Revelation 21:1–5). But we miss out if we're only waiting for that. There are so many ways that we can use our status as his children and his name and authority whilst we are here on earth too.

Here's a picture of what that looks like. Outside my kids' school there is a lollipop man called Chris. When he steps out in front of traffic, cars stop. This is not because they are afraid of him! He's elderly and very friendly. Frankly, any car could mow him down. But they don't. They stop not because of his strength but because he has been given authority. This requires other people to pay attention. His uniform and the way that he steps out gives him backing that is far greater than his own personal strength. Being God's child is a bit like that. In Paul's letter to the Ephesians, he describes some of the gifts God gives us as being like an armour that we can wear to protect and help us (Ephesians 6:10–20). Before it lists all the different pieces of armour, it says, 'Be strong in the Lord and in his mighty power.' We don't need to be strong on our own but can rely on God's strength and what he's given us. He covers us in a sort of clothing that says, 'This is my child, they speak and stand with my authority and strength.'

The lollipop man still has a role to play. If he stays on the pavement, watching the cars go past, they won't stop for him. When he chooses to step out, backed by the authority of his uniform and role, he makes a difference and helps people. We also have to choose to step out. We won't see anything happen if we stay on the sidelines. In Luke 10:1–24, we read about Jesus sending out 72 people to keep doing what he has been doing. They come back amazed at what they can do with his power and authority. He says, 'I have given you authority to trample on snakes and scorpions and to overcome all the power of the enemy; nothing will harm you.' With this authority comes protection. God asks us to do difficult things, but he doesn't leave us alone. He promises to be with us and protect us as we do those things.

So how do we step out? What should we be doing and asking for in Jesus' name? We can see lots of examples from the way that Jesus teaches his disciples. He says, 'In my name they will drive out demons; they will speak in new tongues; they will pick up snakes with their hands; and when they drink deadly poison, it will not hurt them at all; they will place their hands on people who are ill, and they will get well' (Mark 16:17–18). In short, we have authority to do the things that Jesus did whilst he was here on earth. To carry on God's work of helping and healing people. Of bringing his kingdom here on earth, as it is in heaven. As we've already seen, this may not always happen in the way that we hope or expect. But many of us are scared to try or don't realise we can. We need to learn to take a risk, to step out and trust God's strength. Like the lollipop man when he steps out in front of the cars. We see a great example of this in Acts 3. Peter speaks to a man who can't walk and says, 'In the name of Jesus Christ of Nazareth, walk', and he does!

When we hear stories like that, we might think, 'I would never be brave enough to do something like that. What if the person isn't healed and I get laughed at?' It's tempting to hide away and keep a low profile, but we don't need to be afraid. I have a friend called Steve who likes to remind people that success is about trying. It's not about what happens next, it's about stepping out. Not every person we pray for will get healed, but if we don't try, then no one will! God asks us to step out and use his name to help bring what he wants in the world. So we are obedient as his children if we do that. What happens next is up to him. We won't always understand why some people get healed and others don't. Why some prayers are answered in the way that we'd like, and some appear unanswered or to get a different answer. He still asks us to play our part and use what he's given us; to help other people and be part of changing and improving the world. Let's be brave and use all the resources available to us and the authority and power that comes with being his child to see people's lives changed. As we do that, we also open up the opportunity for them to choose to become his child too.

Questions to explore:

1 How do you feel about using Jesus' name to pray for things?

2 When do you use the authority that Jesus has given you? If you haven't before, can you think of an opportunity where you could try?

Ideas of things to try as God's child:

- Choose a Bible verse or two, from this chapter or the small group notes, that reminds you what is available to you as God's child. Learn it or put it somewhere that you will see it regularly. Remind yourself of it when you feel weak or tired.

● Ask God, 'Where do you want me to use your name and your power and authority today?' He may give you a feeling, picture, thought, word or idea at the time. It may be later in the day where you feel a nudge to step out and try doing something you wouldn't normally do.

● Think about something that you think is unjust or unfair. It might be something you see on the news, an issue in your workplace or a friendship challenge for one of your children. Pray for it to change using Jesus' name.

● Try it out. When you see something that's not right, use Jesus' name and authority to ask for change. For example, if you see someone in pain, say, 'Pain leave, in Jesus' name.' Be open to see what happens. If you feel nervous about trying this with other people, experiment on your own or with your family.

✳ ✳ ✳ ✳ ✳ ✳ ✳ ✳ ✳ ✳ ✳ ✳ ✳ ✳ ✳ ✳ ✳ ✳ ✳

NEXT STEPS

Whether you've dipped into one or two, or explored all ten of these ideas, I hope and pray that they've helped you deepen your own relationship with God. This relationship will sustain you in everything you do. Keep investing time and energy in discovering and deepening it. The more we do that, the more we become like him. It enables us to do far more than if we try to do life on our own.

As we invest time and energy in our relationship with God, we will naturally also want our children to do the same. God is their parent too. He is not their grandparent; that is, they don't need to come through us to access God. But we have the amazing joy and privilege of showing them and sharing with them what it means to meet and know him.

The next section, 'Ideas to use with your children', builds on the ways of relating to God that we explored in each chapter. It suggests how you could introduce each of those ideas to your children too. You might want to re-read the relevant chapter and then dip into them. They are only a starting point, so be selective and adapt them so they work for your family. Use them as inspiration for your own ideas.

Although we may find it natural and easy to share most of our passions, interests and relationships with our children, we can freeze or overthink it when it comes to sharing our relationship with God. We can fear being too pushy or forcing ideas and opinions on them. Or we don't know how to do it or feel like we don't have the time, confidence or skills. It doesn't need to be complicated or confusing. God made it to be a normal and natural part of everyday life.

Rachel Turner, the founder of Parenting for Faith, started this ministry to help busy parents and carers like you, to help their children and teens meet and know God throughout every day. Parenting for Faith has hundreds of resources, from courses and podcasts to books and articles. They are all based around five Key Tools and applying them to any situation that you and your family face. They don't require any preparation or complex theological study. You don't need to find any extra time to do more activities. They are just tools for you to use as you go about your normal, everyday life with your children. Many of them are tweaks to things you are already doing. As you read and experiment with the ideas in the next chapter, you will probably find you have already been using them without even knowing it.

Here is a brief summary of each of the tools. You can find out more by going to **parentingforfaith.org/tools**. There you'll find a short video, a simple description, ideas of things to try and answers to frequently asked questions for each tool.

The tools are:

Creating Windows

 This tool builds on the way God has designed our brains to learn best – by watching and trying things for ourselves. It allows kids to glimpse what your relationship with God looks like, so they can learn how to have a real two-way connection with him themselves.

Framing

 Framing is all about explaining – what God is doing, why things happen, who he is. It shows kids how God works in all of life, how to explore the Bible well and work through any questions they might have.

Unwinding

 This is an important tool for helping kids to grow a balanced and healthy view of God. It can be easy to slip into a lopsided view. This tool helps to gently unwind misconceptions, building in a broad and balanced understanding of who God is.

Chat and Catch

This tool encourages children in prayer and hearing God's voice – chatting to him about everything that is on their hearts and catching his response, however he chooses to speak. It helps children to connect directly with God at any time, in all circumstances, wherever they are.

Surfing the Waves

This tool helps us spot what God is doing in a child's life. All children are different, and God's purposes for them are different. Learn to identify their 'waves' and support them as interests and passions come and go.

To learn more about these tools and the many other resources available from Parenting for Faith, head to the website, listen to the podcast or follow on social media.

 facebook.com/parentingforfaithBRF

 twitter.com/godconnected

 instagram.com/parentingforfaithbrf

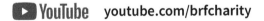 youtube.com/brfcharity

I hope and pray that this book has helped you take some more steps on your journey, and that in the months and years ahead there are plenty more steps. I hope and pray that you'll keep on exploring new ways to live as God's child and help the children in your life to do that too.

IDEAS TO USE WITH YOUR CHILDREN

Idea 1 – Spend time with him

- Talk about God and how he's with you when you're going about your normal day-to-day life. When your child is excited about something, congratulate and celebrate with them and share it with God too.

- Talk to God out loud when your children or teenagers are around. This can be as simple as saying, 'God, please make [insert name] better' when you get a text from a friend who's ill, or, 'Thanks for helping me today, God.'

- Share with your child how you are experimenting with connecting with God (as part of a routine, spontaneously throughout the day or setting time aside). Share with them how you find it. Tell them what helps you feel close to God or reminds you that he's there. How do you feel before or afterwards?

- Incorporate ways for them to try those different methods of connecting with God. For example, if you want to try connecting through a routine, you could suggest, 'Okay, every time we put our shoes on, let's ask God to be with us today.' If you want to focus on spontaneous connection, you could pause when you're in the middle of something else and say, 'Hey, let's tell God something we found funny recently.' If you want to try a scheduled time for connection, you could put the Bible or a devotional book on the breakfast table the night before and read from it as you're eating breakfast the next morning. Those specific examples might not work for your family. Think about when are good times for you and them, and then what might help them to connect.

- For more ideas of how to let your children or teenagers see, hear or notice and how to explain this to them, go to **parentingforfaith.org/creating-windows** and **parentingforfaith.org/framing**.

Idea 2 – Ask lots of questions

- If it's not too personal, write down a question you've asked God and leave it somewhere that your child or teenager can find it. They may or may not notice it, and may not say anything about it. If they do ask you about it, explain what you wrote and why. You could share how you found the experience of asking God a question and how you felt he responded.

- Ask your child lots of questions – open-ended questions with no right answer. Share that you love exploring questions with them and that you are trying to ask God more questions too.

- Ask if they have any questions that they'd like to ask God. Do the same thing as you did on your own. Write it down or ask it to God and then notice any words, pictures, ideas, thoughts or feelings that pop into your mind or body. Chat together about what these might mean and if they match up with what you know about God from the Bible.

- Next time you or your child has a question, try taking it through the four simple steps that Rachel Turner suggests in the Parenting for Faith course: 1) What do you think? 2) What do we know? 3) What do we not know? 4) Share how you've handled it. You can use these steps on your own, to help you explore your own questions and then feed back and share with your child. Or you can use it with your child or teenager to explore the questions that they ask. For a video, downloadable postcard reminder and more information on this, go to **parentingforfaith.org/ post/questions**.

  1 Ask, 'What do you think?' If you're exploring your child's question, find out where they are on the subject, what they already know and what has sparked the question. If you're asking the question, you can do the same thing for yourself – Why are you interested in this? Do you already have a view? Be honest with yourself about your starting point.

  2 Ask, 'What do we know?' Depending on the question, you may already have some of the answer. According to the Bible and wise people around you, what do you already know which will help you answer the question? You might want to look some things up or ask a friend.

3 Ask, 'What do we not know?' Whilst some questions have clear-cut answers, often there are elements that we can't be sure about. Be honest about what you don't know. You might be able to research more. You might feel that God responds to you by showing or reminding you of something. It might be something that remains unanswered for now. That's okay. Park it.

4 Share how you've handled it. You don't need to do this step if you're exploring your own questions with God. But if your child is asking about a certain issue or subject area, share any personal opinions and views you have and why. If it relates to an experience you've had or something you've read or watched, share what those things were and how they influenced you. This helps your child or teenager learn more about you. It also models for them that it's okay to still be forming an opinion on something. It shows them how to go about finding out more about something and weighing up different information and experiences as you go along.

Idea 3 – Mess up but don't give up

- Next time you mess up in front of your child, make a point of stopping and saying sorry. Say this to them if it's affected them. If you need to say sorry to God too, do that out loud there and then or tell them that you're going to chat to God about this later when you reflect on the day.

- Think of some phrases that you can use to keep sharing the message that it's okay to make mistakes. It will be different for every family. For example: 'I made a mistake, everyone makes mistakes sometimes'; 'Getting it wrong is part of learning'; or 'I got it wrong this time and that's okay.'

- Share a story from the past where you made a mistake. Explain how you handled it and what it felt like or what changed if you brought it to God.

- Explain that they can tell God about any mistake or bad choice they've made and nothing will separate them from his love. Encourage them to do that without involving you. You don't need to know and you're not asking them to get information. You can give examples from your own life but then leave them to it.

- Share with them the whole story of the Bible and God's relationship with sin. You could use a storybook retelling, like *The Garden, the Curtain and the Cross* by Carl Laferton (The Good Book Company, 2016), or get some guidance on explaining it in your own words from the Parenting for Faith website at **parentingforfaith.org/post/telling-the-whole-story-facebook-live.**

Idea 4 – Share your emotions

- Name your emotions out loud when your children are around. This could be in the moment or you could share something that happened earlier in the day. For example, 'Earlier when I cut myself doing the washing up, I felt frustrated and told God about it. I told him about how much it hurt and how annoyed I was at myself for not remembering I'd put a knife in there.'

- Try asking questions to help your child understand how they are feeling. Ask them: does it feel more like this or like that? A list of emotion words can also be useful here.

- When you're reading a Bible story, make a game of spotting any time you see an emotion. Use it to chat to God. If you spot someone feeling frustrated, tell God about something you find frustrating. If you spot someone feeling disappointed, use this as a prompt to share some of your disappointments with him.

- Give ideas of things to tell God about or questions to ask him that involve feelings. This could be things like:
  - Tell God about a time when you felt scared.
  - Ask God what makes him feel sad.
  - Tell God where you feel the most comfortable.
  - Ask him what makes him feel especially proud of you.
  - Share with him something that you found funny.

Idea 5 – Ask for help and for what you need

- Leave out your list of things God provided for you, somewhere your children can see it. If they ask about it, share what it is. You could tell them more about some of the situations or circumstances. If it feels natural, you may want to ask if they'd like to try doing the same thing. They could draw or take pictures instead of writing.

- Next time you ask God for something, try doing it out loud so your children can hear.

- Tell them a story about a time when God provided for you or someone you know. If it's someone else's story, you could ask them to share it over dinner or when they're on a video call.

- Write or print out Philippians 4:19 and put it somewhere you'll see it often. Use it as a prompt to ask God aloud for what you need or to encourage your children to do that.

Idea 6 – Appreciate and celebrate

- Do any of the things from the 'Ideas of things to try' section somewhere that your child can see or hear you doing them.

- Notice when your child manages to do something new or that they often struggle with. See if you can think about all the different ways God was involved in that or made it possible. For example, if they got one more mark on the spelling test this week, you could thank him for the amazing way that he made their brain, for teachers and schools, for words, for pens and paper. If they were awarded a swimming badge, you could thank him for water, for swimming pools, for your arms and legs and the way they move. Find out more about how they work. Try to think outside the box in terms of who or what was involved and notice details that you haven't spotted before.

- Experiment with making it part of your family's routine to thank God. It could be part of going to school, going to bed or sharing a meal. Share something you're grateful for, excited about or proud of. Include talking to God, not just each other, about it.

- Are there any creative ways you could include God in your celebrations and successes? Could you ask God for ideas for what to buy or make someone as a birthday present and share you did that? What about getting Jesus a cake or a present on Christmas Day?

Idea 7 – Let him love, comfort and protect you

- Read Psalm 91 together or share those pictures of God being like a castle, a bird or a shield. Ask which one(s) stand out to them as a way to remember God as a safe place of protection.

- When you comfort or protect your child, take the opportunity to share with them that God does those things for them as well. You could take it a step further and share that the most amazing thing about God's love, care and protection is that he is always with us. Explain that as they grow up there will be more and more times where you won't physically be there (at nursery, school or friends' houses, for example). Parents are also human and can misunderstand, get it wrong or be busy with other things. But God is always available and always listening. Encourage them to tell him what they need anytime, anywhere.

- Next time you notice they are in pain or distress, ask, 'Are your feelings or your body hurt?' Ask if they would like to show or tell God what they need and how it feels.

Idea 8 – Learn from him

- Do some research on different learning styles. If this is new to you, it's the perfect opportunity for you to learn something too! Ask your children how they like to learn. Share about how you think you best like to learn.

- Do your Bible reading or listening somewhere they can see or hear you doing it. Share with them how you're experimenting with it. You could make them part of the experiment, such as by getting them to ask you what you learnt later in the day.

- Try doing something new that neither of you have ever done before or going somewhere that neither of you have been. Chat about what you're seeing and experiencing and learning and share that with God too.

- Ask them what they've learnt from God or about him.

Idea 9 – Join in with what he's doing

- If you try getting involved with something new, chat to your child about what inspired you to try that and how you're finding it. If appropriate, invite them to be a part of that too or to find their own way of contributing.

- Spot when they express an interest or dissatisfaction with something in the world. Ask them questions about it and equip them with some next steps to see what joining in could look like. It could be collecting tins for the food bank, getting you better organised to recycle at home, or getting involved with a charity or campaign that they feel particularly drawn to supporting.

- Ask questions to help them explore how they might join in with what God is doing. This could be things like:
  - What annoys you about the world/your school/this area that you think should change?
  - What stands out to you as you watch or read the news?
  - If you had £1,000 to make a difference, what would you use it for?

- Point out things they can do, choices they can make and things they can say that are part of joining in with what God is doing. Try not to direct this and tell them what to do, but just make them aware where they have choices. Feed back to them how their words or actions have helped other people. Encourage them that they are playing their part in something much bigger and won't always see the full effect. For example, if they choose to talk to and play with a child who is lonely, say, 'I saw what you did there. God doesn't want anyone to feel alone, and you noticed they were by themselves and helped God by making sure they had a friend to play with. He loves it when you join in with him like that.'

Idea 10 – Use the family name

- Ask your child or teenager what they like about being part of your family and what they like about being part of God's family. You're not looking for 'right' answers but to start a conversation to explore what those things mean to them. Share your responses to those questions too.

- Try using God's name and authority somewhere that your child can hear you do that. For example, you could ask for someone to be healed in Jesus' name. If they're not there at the time, tell them about it afterwards. Be honest if this is a new experience for you and you're feeling unsure about it. How did it feel? How did God respond or the situation change? What were you excited or scared about?

- Ask them what they are most looking forward to about heaven. If you don't know much about it, you could read some of Revelation in the Bible. You could also do some 'chat and catch' telling God the things you are looking forward to and asking him questions about what it will be like. Find out more about what 'chat and catch' is and how to use this tool with your children at **parentingforfaith.org/tool/chat-and-catch**.

✳ ✳ ✳ ✳ ✳ ✳ ✳ ✳ ✳ ✳ ✳ ✳ ✳ ✳ ✳ ✳ ✳ ✳ ✳

SMALL GROUP NOTES

It can be helpful to explore this kind of material together, bouncing ideas off one another. This could be with a partner or a friend or two; you could start a new group or use this book in a group that you already attend. Play around to find what works best in your context. These are outlines of potential sessions which you can adapt.

The timings give you a rough guide of how long different sections might take. The size of your group and whether you are meeting online or in person will affect how long to spend on each section. You can easily shorten or lengthen them. You don't need to do all the sessions and you don't need to do them in order – for example, you could look just at the opening question and idea, and omit the Bible study and discussion.

The sessions work equally well online or in person. For online gatherings, I'd suggest sticking to the shorter of the suggested timings. People may find it helpful to have their own copy of the book and read through the chapter.

Introduction and the offer

- **Gathering** (5–15 mins). Start with a chance to chat and get to know each other or catch up (and refreshments if in person).

- **Introduction** (10–15 mins). Welcome, explain how the group will work and ask people to introduce themselves. It can be helpful to hear about the children in people's lives and what they hope to get from the group in the first session.

- **Share key ideas** (5–10 mins). Read or summarise the introduction (page 6) and the offer (page 9) at the start of the book. Ask people what stood out to them. What did they agree or disagree with, and why? *Key ideas to explore:*
  - Having children can be a busy stage of life where it can be hard to find time to connect with God. But our children and our relationship with them can actually help us grow to know God better.

- You don't have to have it all figured out – part of being a child is that you're known and loved for exactly who you are. Relating to God as his child looks different for everyone.
- God invites us to be his children. It's not something he forces on us. If we choose to say yes to that, it's a two-way commitment.
- God isn't like people. He is a perfect parent. Our view of him is shaped by many things – we weren't parented perfectly and we don't parent perfectly. The ideas we explore are just illustrations. (Please be very sensitive to the range of backgrounds and situations in your group.)

- **Bible study questions** (10–15 mins). You may want to do one, several or all of these. See what sparks people's interest and helps the discussion.
  - Read John 1:1–13. *What does being a child of God mean to you?*
  - Read Psalm 68:4–6. *What does it mean to be 'a father to the fatherless'? How does he set 'the lonely in families'?*
  - Read Psalm 103:13–18. *How does a father have compassion on his children? What does it mean for God to do that with us?*
  - Read Matthew 19:13–15. *Why did Jesus correct his disciples? What can we learn from these children?*

- **Follow-up question** (5 mins). *In what ways can we be like children with God?* If people are struggling, look at some of the titles of future chapters to start you off.

- **Pray together** (10–15 mins). Ask if people have any prayer requests and pray for each other.

Idea 1 – Spend time together

- **Gathering** (5–15 mins). Start with a chance to chat (and refreshments if in person).

- **Welcome and recap** (5–10 mins). Welcome, introduce anyone new, recap the previous session and ask if anyone has any more thoughts about that.

- **Opening question and idea** (5–10 mins). *Think about your relationship with your child(ren). What has helped that relationship grow and get stronger?* If people are struggling for ideas, you could suggest some from the chapter and ask people what that looks like for them. For example, what memories have they made with their child(ren)? Just as we do all these things with our children, so we can do all these things with God as his child too. Yet so many of us miss out by keeping God for Christmas and crises.

- **Bible study questions** (5–10 mins). You may want to do one or both of these. See what sparks people's interest and helps the discussion.
  - Read Psalm 139:1–18. *What stands out to you? How does it feel to be fully known by God?*
  - Read John 14:15–27. *Do you feel that God, by his Holy Spirit, is always with you? What difference does that make to you?*

- **Further discussion** (5–10 mins). Share the coffee analogy on pages 13–14. *Which one(s) best describe how you like to spend time with God at the moment?* As part of that, you might want to explore why that works for them and ask if they are open to trying the other ideas too.

- **Individual reflection** (5 mins). Ask the questions from the 'Questions to explore' section on page 15. Give people some time and space to reflect on their own. You might like to provide pens and paper and play some music. People may like to feed back or keep these reflections private.

- **Getting practical** (5–10 mins). Ask people to think of one thing they would like to try this week. You can use the suggestions at the end of the chapter for ideas. Some groups may also want to think about how to help their children spend time with God too. There are ideas for this in the 'Ideas to use with your children' section (page 66). They may want to make a note of this in their phone or in their book as a reminder. Stress that this isn't homework: if they don't do it, that's not a problem! Sometimes it's helpful to have something practical to take away to help put into practice what you've explored.

- **Pray together** (10–15 mins). Ask if people have any prayer requests and pray for each other.

Idea 2 – Ask lots of questions

- **Gathering** (5–15 mins). Start with a chance to chat (and refreshments if in person).

- **Welcome and recap** (5–10 mins). Welcome and introduce anyone new. Recap the previous session. Ask if anyone experimented with trying a different way to connect with God (think back to the analogy of the ways people drink).

- **Opening questions and ideas** (5–10 mins). *What sort of questions do your children ask you?* People might want to give examples. *Do you think asking and answering questions helps your relationship with your child? How?* Share some of the different ways that the chapter suggests questions can strengthen a relationship. We can experience these benefits with God as his child. If you have time, you could also ask *Why do we stop asking questions?*

- **Bible study questions** (10–15 mins). You may want to do one, several or all of these. See what sparks people's interest and helps the discussion.
  - Read Jeremiah 33:3. *What sort of things does God want to tell us? How can we start that conversation?*
  - Read Habakkuk 1—2 or watch an overview of Habakkuk from the Bible Project at **bibleproject.com/explore/video/habakkuk**. *What's going on here? How does God respond to Habakkuk's questions?*
  - Open up the book of Psalms and see if you can find any questions. *Why do you think David asks so many questions? What do they tell us about his relationship with God?*

- **Exploring answering questions** (10–15 mins). Introduce the idea of four steps to answering any question. You can get a video and downloadable version of this at **parentingforfaith.org/post/questions**. Talk about how they might use it for their own questions and their children's questions. You might want to pick a real-life example of a question someone has or their child has and work through it together.

- **Individual reflection** (5 mins). Ask the questions from the 'Questions to explore' section on page 21. Give people some time and space to reflect on their own. You might like to provide pens and paper and play some music. People may like to feed back or keep these reflections private.

- **Getting practical** (5–10 mins). Ask people to think of one thing they would like to try this week. You can use the suggestions at the end of the chapter for ideas. Some groups may also want to think about how to help their children spend time with God too. There are ideas for this in the 'Ideas to use with your children' section (page 66).

- **Pray together** (10–15 mins). Ask if people have any prayer requests and pray for each other.

Idea 3 – Mess up but don't give up

- **Gathering** (5–15 mins). Start with a chance to chat (and refreshments if in person).

- **Welcome and recap** (5–10 mins). Welcome and introduce anyone new. Recap the previous session. Ask if anyone has asked God any questions over the last week or thought about question-asking differently.

- **Opening question and idea** (5–10 mins). There is a podcast called 'How To Fail' with Elizabeth Day, in which famous people share three of their failures. They can be big or small, funny or serious. *If you were on the podcast, which failure(s) would you share?* Share the idea that kids make mistakes all the time but don't give up on what they are trying to learn. As adults we can be embarrassed or ashamed of our mistakes and beat ourselves up about them or try to hide them. That's not what God wants for us. He wants us to come to him, wherever we are and whatever has happened.

- **Bible study questions** (10–15 mins). You may want to do one, several or all of these. See what sparks people's interest and helps the discussion.
    - Read 1 John 1:8—2:1. *In what ways do we deceive ourselves (verse 8)?* and/or *What does his promise of forgiving us our sins and purifying us from all unrighteousness mean? What does that feel like to us?*
    - Read James 5:16–18. *Do you share with other people areas in which you struggle? If you have done so in the past, what difference has that made?*
    - Read Psalm 51:1–12. *Which parts of this psalm stand out to you or reflect your own experience of saying sorry to God?*
    - Read Matthew 6:9–13. *Do you find it easy to forgive others? What makes it challenging?*

- **Follow-on activity** (10–15 mins). Introduce the idea of a daily examen and/or share the five apology languages.

Daily examen

Ask the group to get comfortable and close their eyes and talk them through the following steps. This is an idea that Ignatius Loyola came up with, more than 400 years ago, as a way of prayerfully reflecting on the day.

- Become aware of God's presence. Let him know you're thinking about him and ask him to help you think back over the day.
- Review the day with gratitude. Say thanks for all the good things, big or small, that were a part of your day.
- Pay attention to your emotions. Reflect on the different feelings you experienced through the day, and ask God to show you what he might be saying or what your emotions might be showing you. Ask him to show you anywhere you messed up or anything that you need to say sorry for. As they come to mind, say sorry and thank God for forgiving you. As simple as that.
- Choose one feature of the day and pray about it. Focus on one thing that stands out to you – a feeling, a moment, an interaction – and chat to God about it.
- Look forward to tomorrow. Ask God for his help for whatever you're facing tomorrow.

Share that if people want to use this, they don't have to stick to this exact pattern, but it can be a useful starting point for developing your own version.

Five apology languages

Share that we all apologise and like to be apologised to in different ways. In their book *The Five Apology Languages* (Moody Publishers, 2022), Gary Chapman and Jennifer Thomas suggest five different ways to say sorry:

- Express regret: 'I'm sorry.'
- Accept responsibility: 'I was wrong.'
- Make restitution: 'How can I make it right?'
- Plan for change: 'I'll take steps to prevent a recurrence.'
- Request forgiveness: 'Can you find it in your heart to…?'

Ask the group which ones they tend to focus on when they apologise. Is it different for saying sorry to God than to other people?

- **Individual reflection** (5 mins). Ask the questions from the 'Questions to explore' section on page 27. Give people some time and space to reflect on their own. You might like to provide pens and paper and play some music. People may like to feed back or keep these reflections private.

- **Getting practical** (5–10 mins). Ask people to think of one thing they would like to try this week. You can use the suggestions at the end of the chapter for ideas. Some groups may also want to think about how to help their children spend time with God too. There are ideas for this in the 'Ideas to use with your children' section (page 66).

- **Pray together** (10–15 mins). Ask if people have any prayer requests and pray for each other.

Idea 4 – Share your emotions

- **Gathering** (5–15 mins). Start with a chance to chat (and refreshments if in person).

- **Welcome and recap** (5–10 mins). Welcome and introduce anyone new. Recap the previous session. Ask if anyone has thought differently about mess-ups, mistakes and saying sorry this week.

- **Opening questions and ideas** (5–10 mins). *What is your experience of recognising and sharing your emotions? How do you work out what you are feeling? Who do you share that with? Nobody? A spouse or friend? God?* Discuss the idea that children tend to be very good at expressing their emotions, but as adults we tend to repress or try to hide them. We can learn to recognise our emotions and share them with God, who as our loving parent can handle whatever we are feeling.

- **Bible study questions** (10–15 mins). You may want to do one, two or all three of these. See what sparks people's interest and helps the discussion.
  - Read Ecclesiastes 3:1–4. *What season are you in now or what seasons have you been in recently?*
  - Read Psalm 7:9 and 62:8. *What do these verses tell us about how God sees our emotions?*
  - Romans 12:15–16. *How can we help each other with our emotions?*

- **Individual reflection** (5–10 mins). Ask the questions from the 'Questions to explore' section on page 31. Give people some time and space to reflect on their own. You might like to give some extra time to this section for this session. Print out some emotion lists (google 'emotion lists' and you will get lots of free examples). Invite people to circle the ones that express how they are feeling. Alternatively, you could look at the suggestions of psalms to read when you are experiencing a particular emotion on page 32. Give people time to read one and highlight or write down the bits that resonate with them.

- **Getting practical** (5–10 mins). Ask people to think of one thing they would like to try this week. You can use the suggestions at the end of the chapter for ideas. Some groups may also want to think about how to help their children spend time with God too. There are ideas for this in the 'Ideas to use with your children' section (page 66).

- **Pray together** (10–15 mins). Ask if people have any prayer requests and pray for each other.

Idea 5 – Ask for help and for what you need

- **Gathering** (5–15 mins). Start with a chance to chat (and refreshments if in person).

- **Welcome and recap** (5–10 mins). Welcome and introduce anyone new. Recap the previous session. Ask if anyone has been more aware of recognising or sharing their emotions this week or helping their child with this.

- **Opening questions and ideas** (5–10 mins). *When you become a parent, what job titles or roles do you gain?* You could give some examples like taxi driver or cook. *Do you have any stories of asking God for something? That could be you or someone else. What happened?* Share the idea that God takes on many roles as our parent, just as we do for our children. He can be our healer, protector, provider, comforter and so on. He is a good Father who wants to give us good things and he invites us to ask for what we need.

- **Bible study questions** (10–15 mins). You may want to do one or both of these. See what sparks people's interest and helps the discussion.
  - Read Matthew 6:19–34. *What stands out to you? Which parts of that do you find it hardest to believe or live with?*
  - Read 1 Kings 17. *Have you ever been scared of doing something or going somewhere because you weren't sure how God would provide for you? Have you ever had opportunities to share what he's done for you or help other people too?*

- **Individual reflection** (5 mins). Ask the questions from the 'Questions to explore' section on page 36. Give people some time and space to reflect on their own. You might like to provide pens and paper and play some music. People may like to feed back or keep these reflections private.

- **Getting practical** (5–10 mins). Ask people to think of one thing they would like to try this week. You can use the suggestions at the end of the chapter for ideas. Some groups may also want to think about how to help their children spend time with God too. There are ideas for this in the 'Ideas to use with your children' section (page 66).

- **Pray together** (10–15 mins). Ask if people have any prayer requests and pray for each other. Remind them to be bold and ask for anything that they need, however small or insignificant it may sound to other people.

Idea 6 – Appreciate and celebrate

- **Gathering** (5–15 mins). Start with a chance to chat (and refreshments if in person).

- **Welcome and recap** (5–10 mins). Welcome and introduce anyone new. Recap the previous session. Ask if anyone has asked God for anything this week and how that went.

- **Opening questions and ideas** (5–10 mins). *What have your children noticed and enjoyed recently?* Share the idea that children notice and delight in things that we sometimes miss or don't notice as adults. God loves it when we notice and enjoy all that he has given us and loves to see us enjoy those things and hear our thanks. *What have you or your children done recently that you've celebrated or been proud of them for?* After people have shared, ask *How do we feel about sharing and celebrating our own achievements? Was it easier to share about your child?* As a parent, many of the things that we do go unseen and uncelebrated, but God, our parent, wants to celebrate with us. He is proud of us.

- **Bible study questions** (10–15 mins). You may want to do one, two or all three of these. See what sparks people's interest and helps the discussion.
  - Read 2 Chronicles 20:5–20. *What stands out to you about the way Jehoshaphat approached this situation? Have you ever thanked and praised God even in the middle of a difficult situation? What happened?*
  - Read Luke 17:11–19. *Why do you think Luke told this story? Can you think of situations where you are more like the nine who carried on? What about situations where you are like the one who returned to Jesus? What draws us back to say thank you or make us forget and carry on?*
  - Talk about the different situations of Hannah and Mary. Hannah prayed for a child and God answered by sending her one. Mary found herself unexpectedly pregnant. Both chose to thank and praise God. You can read about them in 1 Samuel 2:1–10 and Luke 1:46–55. *Has something similar happened in your life? Where have you thanked and praised God for answering something you asked for? Where have you thanked and praised him for something unexpected?*

- **Individual reflection** (5 mins). Ask the questions from the 'Questions to explore' section on page 42. Give people some time and space to reflect on their own. You might like to provide pens and paper and play some music. People may like to feed back or keep these reflections private.

- **Getting practical** (5–10 mins). Ask people to think of one thing they would like to try this week. You can use the suggestions at the end of the chapter for ideas. Some groups may also want to think about how to help their children spend time with God too. There are ideas for this in the 'Ideas to use with your children' section (page 66).

- **Pray together** (10–15 mins). Ask if people have any prayer requests and pray for each other. You might like to particularly focus on sharing things that you can celebrate and appreciate, and thank God for those together.

Idea 7 – Let him love, comfort and protect you

- **Gathering** (5–15 mins). Start with a chance to chat (and refreshments if in person).

- **Welcome and recap** (5–10 mins). Welcome and introduce anyone new. Recap the previous session. Ask if anyone has anything to celebrate or be grateful for this week.

- **Opening questions and ideas** (5–10 mins). *What does your child need to help them feel loved, safe and secure?* Introduce the idea that to thrive all humans need emotional connections as well as their physical needs met. Not everyone will have experienced this in their childhood, or feel confident to know how to provide this for their children. But we can always be confident that God is available to meet our every need. He is a trustworthy and safe place to form a secure attachment. *What helps you to feel loved, safe and secure? Is God a part of that?*

- **Bible study questions** (10–15 mins). You may want to do one, two or all three of these. See what sparks people's interest and helps the discussion.
  - Read Psalm 91. *Which of those illustrations stands out as a helpful picture of God or a way that you relate to him? Do you struggle with any of them?*
  - Talk about the different experiences of Moses facing the Red Sea while being chased by an army and Daniel's three friends in the fire (along with Daniel himself in the lion's den). God showed his love, comfort and protection in different ways. *Which can you most relate to at the moment?*
  - Read Mark 4:35–41. Explain the boat analogy on page 47. *Do you have examples of those situations in your life or in your children's lives?*

- **Individual reflection** (5 mins). Ask the questions from the 'Questions to explore' section on page 47. Give people some time and space to reflect on their own. You might like to provide pens and paper and play some music. People may like to feed back or keep these reflections private.

- **Getting practical** (5–10 mins). Ask people to think of one thing they would like to try this week. You can use the suggestions at the end of the chapter for ideas. Some groups may also want to think about how to help their children spend time with God too. There are ideas for this in the 'Ideas to use with your children' section (page 66).

- **Pray together** (10–15 mins). Ask if people have any prayer requests and pray for each other. *Be aware that this session may have raised some sensitive issues and people might need follow-up or signposting to other organisations for help or prayer.*

Idea 8 – Learn from him

- **Gathering** (5–15 mins). Start with a chance to chat (and refreshments if in person).

- **Welcome and recap** (5–10 mins). Welcome and introduce anyone new. Recap the previous session. Ask if anyone has been more aware of God's love, comfort or protection over the last week.

- **Opening questions and ideas** (5–10 mins). *What have you learned recently? How do you learn best?* Introduce the idea that we are aware of our children learning all the time but as adults it can be tempting to think we know all that we need to. We can also get lazy about where we learn from. We end up learning from the social media we scroll through or the TV we watch rather than choosing to learn from places and people that help us. *How can we learn from God?* You might want to look at the four ways discussed in the chapter.

- **Bible study questions** (10–15 mins). You may want to do one, two or all three of these. See what sparks people's interest and helps the discussion.
    - Read 1 Kings 3:5–10. *If you were Solomon, what would you have asked for? What do you think it means to be given wisdom from God?*
    - Read Philippians 4:9. *Which other Christians do you copy or learn from? What is it about them that makes you want to learn from them?*
    - Read Psalm 32:8. *What does God instructing and teaching you mean to you? Do you have any examples of what it has looked like in your life or the lives of people you know?*

- **Individual reflection** (5 mins). Ask the questions from the 'Questions to explore' section on page 53. Give people some time and space to reflect on their own. You might like to provide pens and paper and play some music. People may like to feed back or keep these reflections private.

- **Getting practical** (5–10 mins). Ask people to think of one thing they would like to try this week. You can use the suggestions at the end of the chapter for ideas. Some groups may also want to think about how to help their children spend time with God too. There are ideas for this in the 'Ideas to use with your children' section (page 66).

- **Pray together** (10–15 mins). Ask if people have any prayer requests and pray for each other.

Idea 9 – Join in with what he's doing

- **Gathering** (5–15 mins). Start with a chance to chat (and refreshments if in person).

- **Welcome and recap** (5–10 mins). Welcome and introduce anyone new. Recap the previous session. Ask if anyone has tried a different way to learn this week.

- **Opening questions and ideas** (5–10 mins). *When you were a child, when did you join in with something that your parent was doing?* Share the idea that children often join in with what their parents are doing. God, our parent, is at work helping people and transforming the world, and he invites us to be a part of that. *How do you feel you join in with this, or how would you like to?*

- **Bible study questions** (10–15 mins). You may want to do one, two or all three of these. See what sparks people's interest and helps the discussion.
  - Read John 5. *Why did Jesus take the risk of healing the man on the sabbath even though he knew the religious leaders would be unhappy with that? Do you ever feel like joining in with what God is doing involves taking risks for you too?*
  - Read Matthew 25:35–40. *Which of those things are you already involved in or can see yourself getting involved in? Which seem offputting or uncomfortable and what might change how you feel about them?*

- Read the Lord's Prayer in Matthew 6:9–13. Notice the order that Jesus suggests in that model prayer. *Is this the order we tend to pray for things in? What does praying for God's kingdom to come mean to you? What do you think it looks like?*

- **Individual reflection** (5 mins). Ask the questions from the 'Questions to explore' section on page 58. Give people some time and space to reflect on their own. You might like to provide pens and paper and play some music. People may like to feed back or keep these reflections private.

- **Getting practical** (5–10 mins). Ask people to think of one thing they would like to try this week. You can use the suggestions at the end of the chapter for ideas. Some groups may also want to think about how to help their children spend time with God too. There are ideas for this in the 'Ideas to use with your children' section (page 66).

- **Pray together** (10–15 mins). Ask if people have any prayer requests and pray for each other.

Idea 10 – Use the family name

- **Gathering** (5–15 mins). Start with a chance to chat (and refreshments if in person).

- **Welcome and recap** (5–10 mins). Welcome and introduce anyone new. Recap the previous session. Ask if anyone has tried joining in with what God has been doing or thought about it differently.

- **Opening question and idea** (5–10 mins). *Does anyone have any funny/interesting/outrageous stories about their name?* Introduce the analogy of the lollipop man on page 60.

- **Bible study questions** (10–15 mins). You may want to do one, two or all three of these. See what sparks people's interest and helps the discussion.
    - Read Ephesians 6:10–20. *Which of those instructions or pieces of armour most stand out to you as something you need or something you are very aware of?*
    - Read Romans 8:14–30. *What suffering do you think Paul is talking about here? And what future hope? What do you struggle most with about*

being God's child here on earth and what are you most looking forward to about heaven?

- — Read John 14. *What difference does having the Holy Spirit make to us continuing Jesus' work here on earth?*

- **Individual reflection** (5 mins). Ask the questions from the 'Questions to explore' section on page 61. Give people some time and space to reflect on their own. You might like to provide pens and paper and play some music. People may like to feed back or keep these reflections private.

- **Getting practical** (5–10 mins). Ask people to think of one thing they would like to try this week. You can use the suggestions at the end of the chapter for ideas. Some groups may also want to think about how to help their children spend time with God too. There are ideas for this in the 'Ideas to use with your children' section (page 66).

- **Pray together** (10–15 mins). Ask if people have any prayer requests and pray for each other.

- **Next steps** (5 mins). Chat as a group about how you want to stay in touch or what you might like to do next, individually or together.

ACKNOWLEDGEMENTS

To my children, Brielle, Benji and Caitlin Hawken: it is a joy and a privilege to be your mum. Thank you for showing me how to be a child and bearing with me as I learn to be a parent. You inspire and help me every day. Even when I'm grumpy.

To my husband, Matt Hawken: you tirelessly champion, support and encourage me – practically, spiritually and emotionally. Thank you for believing that God can use me and cheering me on to get there. I couldn't do what I do without you.

To my parents, Mike and Charlotte Cashman: thank you for giving me great examples of how to parent and continuing to parent me even though I'm supposed to be a grown-up now. For your extra grandparenting hours whilst I was writing, and for proofreading the final draft.

To the Starbucks girls, Maggie Williams, Iona Richardson, Helen Cairns-Terry and Emily Desborough: thank you for praying with me through the last five years of parenting and life's ups and downs. In the midst of that, you always reminded me of my identity, first and foremost, as God's child.

To the Parenting for Faith team, Rachel Turner, Becky Sedgwick, Kate Irvine and Iona Gray: thank you for teaching me everything I know. You are not just colleagues but also some of my greatest friends. I love being a team with you.

To my friends who helped me edit, Rachel Turner, Caitlin Harland and Becky Sedgwick: thank you for selflessly giving your time and wisdom. For seeing what I couldn't and getting me unstuck. You turned this into a book people could actually read!

To the New Life Church Milton Keynes Small Group, Naomi Artus, Monica and Josiah Clark, Nathan and Katie Kennard, Susannah Quinn and Kylie Tumolo: for being willing guinea pigs to explore this with. You shaped this book and my thinking in so many ways and I really cherished our Thursday nights together.

To Olivia Warburton, Richard Fisher and the rest of the team at BRF: thank you for your support and giving me the opportunity to write. Your hard work behind the scenes is invaluable.

To Bill Lattimer and Caroline Montgomery: thank you for your time and investment in Parenting for Faith over the years and the way you have personally encouraged me.

Last but not least, God, thanks for adopting me as your child. Keep me learning how to fully take up and enjoy that offer every day. Thank you for patiently waiting for me to explore this with you and write this book. Sorry it took me five years to get around to it – I'm still learning!

Enabling all ages to grow in faith

Anna Chaplaincy
Living Faith
Messy Church
Parenting for Faith

BRF is a Christian charity that resources individuals and churches. Our vision is to enable people of all ages to grow in faith and understanding of the Bible and to see more people equipped to exercise their gifts in leadership and ministry.

To find out more about our work, visit

brf.org.uk

Ingram Content Group UK Ltd.
Milton Keynes UK
UKHW020712270723
425883UK00016B/642

9 781800 391987